What People Are Saying About
Patti Smith and This Book

"In *What Am I to Do Now?*, Patti Smith shares how we can overcome situations that might leave us hopeless or in shock and move toward success and happiness one step at a time. Through colorful stories, she illustrates how we can take practical and purposeful actions to achieve our goals. Let her seven-step system reignite your fire so nothing will hold you back."

— Tyler R. Tichelaar, PhD and Award-Winning Author of
Narrow Lives and *The Best Place*

"Patti, your energy, inspiration, and coaching has been the flashlight to help me navigate in the dark, igniting my inner passion and putting it into action. Thank you for being a shining supportive light in my life and providing me with more clarity to become the woman who makes it happen!"

— Tammy Williams, Nutritionist for the City of Los Angeles

"Sometimes life can be difficult. Sometimes things happen that cause us to get stuck or become stagnant. But the truth is that our happiness and success is largely up to us. We may just need someone to light a fire in us to help us move forward. Patti Smith can do just that. In *What Am I to Do Now?*, she shares her Seven Step IgniteU System, which will have you moving toward new beginnings with lightning speed!"

— Nicole Gabriel, Author of *Finding Your Inner Truth*
and *Stepping Into Your Becoming*

"Patti, because of the high-caliber questions you asked me, I was able to shift my perspective and hire more people to help me level up my business."

— Jennifer Hobaica, Owner – Olive U

"I have been Patti Smith's client for four years. Patti has been a steadfast supporter of my vision and my life. She has become a great teacher, mentor, and friend. Patti is a smart, gracious, and generous person who always seeks the very best for her clients. She has a talent and expertise in helping individuals reach their full potential through her teachings on best business practices and spiritual laws. Through her coaching, we have worked on my life vision and on my business practices. I have been able to take the principles I have learned from Patti and immediately apply them to my business and life. I know what I have learned from Patti is also benefiting my clients by making me a better business consultant and, thereby, more profitable. If you are looking to take your business and life to the next level, I highly recommend Patti as a business and spiritual coach."

— Jamie Jackson, Principal/Non-Profit & Small Business Management Consultant

"Patti, I just wanted to share a pic with you of me and Jason. Thank you for helping me to manifest this into my life! This or something better!"

— Maryann Baum, Real Estate Agent

"Patti Smith knows what it is to have life throw you a curveball. From caring for her dying sister to the woes of dating, she has experienced the situations that can make you want to throw in the towel on life, but each time, she listened to her intuition, changed her perspective, and chose to create her own destiny. In *What Am I To Do Now?* she shares what she has learned. Get ready to experience your what's next evolution!"

— Patrick Snow, Publishing Coach and Best-Selling Author of *Creating Your Own Destiny* and *The Affluent Entrepreneur*

"Patti, thank you so much for coming out and speaking at our meeting today. What a powerful topic! You did an amazing job! I know you made an impact on my staff as well. So glad I was able to be there!"

— Tammy Reese, Executive Nutrition Director

WHAT AM I TO DO
NOW?

Simple Strategies to Navigate the Unknown
and IGNITE What's Next in Your Life

Linda,
Celebrate
Your What's
Next Evolution!
Patti Smith ♡

PATTI SMITH

AVIVA
PUBLISHING
New York

WHAT AM I TO DO NOW?
Simple Strategies to Navigate the Unknown and IGNITE What's Next in Your Life

Address all inquiries to:
Patti Smith
Patti@PattiSmithCoaching.com
www.PattiSmithCoaching.com

ISBN: 978-1-63618-245-2
Library of Congress Control Number: 2022923559

Editors: Larry Alexander and Tyler Tichelaar, Superior Book Productions
Cover Design: Nicole Gabriel, Angel Dog Productions
Interior Book Layout: Nicole Gabriel, Angel Dog Productions
Author Photo: Janet Barnett

Every attempt has been made to properly source all quotes.
Printed in the United States of America
First Edition
2 4 6 8 10 12

DEDICATION

To my big sister Marie and my mother, Olga Marie, my very first mentors and now my angels in heaven. I'm on this path because of you and dedicate this book to the both of you.

To my husband Tommy, the love of my life, who's absolutely been my rock and has challenged me to truly be the best I can be. I'm forever grateful for your love and support.

To my daughter Christina, my pride and joy, who's helped me ride my green growing edge (glad it didn't send me over the edge—ha-ha), which also became the kick in the butt I needed to finish this book and ignite my what's next evolution. Your strength and resilience continue to inspire me.

To my father Dimitri, "Don," still going strong at ninety-three. Thank you for *always* being such a good listener. Also, your "mental switch" is genius.

To my li'l sis Carrie, thank you for being my cheerleader (except when we're arguing, of course—ha-ha).

To my li'l bro Larry, thanks for making me laugh so much.

To my big brothers, Jim and Greg, thanks for helping me face my fear of tornados (more like scared it right out of me—ha-ha).

To my dear friend Sherri Nickols, who's been with me through thick and thin, thank you for always encouraging me.

To my niece Caty and nephew Josh—your mom would be so very proud of the beautiful individuals you've both become, as I am.

ACKNOWLEDGMENTS

I would love to express my deepest gratitude to every individual who helped me bring this book into being and supported me on my journey throughout the process. Thank you from the bottom of my heart to:

My entire literary team who helped me through the process of writing and publishing my book. It truly was a labor of love. Thank you Patrick Snow, my book coach, who encouraged me to write a full-blown book and helped me find the belief in myself that I did have it in me to make this happen. Thank you Tyler Tichelaar and Larry Alexander, my editors, who rounded out all the edges of my manuscript and helped me bring everything together in such a seamless manner. Thank you Nicole Gabriel, my book cover and book layout designer. What a great collaboration. I enjoyed the entire creative process with you. Thank you Susan Friedmann for helping me with the final touches of actually getting my book published. Truly an amazing team!

Sam Horn, for your brilliant insight with the book title!

My Dreambuilder and Life Mastery Consultant community—especially Felicia Lonobile, Kevin Smith, Beth Wolfe, Athina Salazar, Eric Bastien, Lisa Houston, Andrea Nardozza, and Janice Bussing.

The five-star staff at the Life Mastery Institute, now the Brave Thinking Institute, as well as the exceptional instruction and ongoing support from Jennifer Jimenez, John Boggs, Matt Boggs, Rich Boggs, Kirsten Wells, and Katie Augustine.

My mastermind partners who continue to support me as true partners in believing, I'm so grateful for your encouragement, accountability and belief in me and my big goals and dreams. Thank you Sherri Nickols, Toni Caruso, Elisa Ellis, and Sarah Buxbaum. Also Brigitta Kyber, who's always been a bright light of encouragement with everything I do.

My eWomen Network, for rallying and inspiring me through the years in my continuing what's next evolution—such an awesome community of entrepreneurial women who "lift as they climb."

Mary Morrissey, Bob Proctor, Felicia Searcy, and Sandra Yancey, thank you for your wisdom, brilliance and mentorship. You always inspire me to elevate into my next best version.

My husband Tommy and daughter Christina, thank you for your patience, input, and being such a special piece of my purpose and my story. I've learned so much from you both and love you more than I can express in words.

"Dreams are the illustrations

from the book your soul

is writing about you."

— Marsha Norman

CONTENTS

Introduction   You Matter   17

PART I   **ESTABLISHING A FOUNDATION**   **23**

Chapter 1   Igniting the Fire of Your Soul   25

Chapter 2   Shifting Your Mindset to What's Possible   37

Chapter 3   Letting Go to Move Forward   51

Chapter 4   Leading Your Life   67

Chapter 5   Connecting With Your Why   83

PART II   **THE 7 STEP SYSTEM FOR LEADING A LIFE THAT LIGHTS YOU UP**   **101**

Chapter 6   1 - Inspire Your Imagination   103

Chapter 7   2 - Get Clear on What You Want and Why   113

Chapter 8   3 - Nail Down Your Decision to Go for It   123

Chapter 9   4 - Invite in Support from Like-Minded   135
                People and Mentors

Chapter 10   5 - Take Inspired Action Every Day   147

Chapter 11   6 - Embrace Gratitude Throughout Your Journey   161

Chapter 12   7 - Unite With a New Self-Image   171

PART III   **BREAKING THROUGH MIND BLOCKS AND ALIGNING**   **183**
                WITH A VISION-DRIVEN LIFE

Chapter 13   Deserving a Life That Inspires You   185

Chapter 14   Trusting Your Intuition   195

Chapter 15   Using Fear as Your Fuel   205

Chapter 16   Reframing Failure as Feedback   215

Chapter 17   Walking Off Life's Stage Is Not an Option   225

Chapter 18   Believing in Yourself   241

Chapter 19   Choosing Happiness and Finding Fulfillment   251

Chapter 20   Living a Vision-Driven Life   263

A Final Note   Igniting Your What's Next Evolution   271

About the Author   279

Book Patti Smith to Speak at Your Next Event   283

Patti Smith Innovative Coaching   285

INTRODUCTION

YOU MATTER

"It does not matter how you came into the world.
What matters is that you are here."

— Oprah Winfrey

As a professional speaker and life success coach, I've spoken with many individuals who are ready to create a new chapter in their lives—one that involves meaningful, fulfilling work that makes a positive difference in the world. I like to call it your *What's Next*, and because it is something you evolve into, it is your *What's Next Evolution*. It is an ever-evolving question that continues to pop up as we navigate change throughout the various stages of our lives.

But you may be wondering, *Where do I even begin?* That is where most people hit a brick wall and stop, instead accepting complacency.

I decided to write this book as a transformational guide to help you navigate the unknown and ignite your what's next evolution—coming from a place of wonder and possibility, no matter where you are or what age you may be.

Our belief in ourselves, in our truth, and in our purpose is a transformational process. We have built into our own authentic nature the desire to grow and expand and, I believe, to do good and make a difference. Young children connect with this natural process so much more easily than adults. What happens is as we start moving around in society, we begin being put into little boxes tied up in pretty bows. On the outside, those boxes may appear beautiful, but on the inside, they can be constricting and suffocating. It's like trying to fit a square peg into a round hole. When we were toddlers, we were encouraged to *dream big* and use our imagination. We were told we could be anything we wanted to be, could go anywhere we wanted to go, and could experience everything we could imagine.

The next phase was when we were ready to start our formal education as developing young humans. The dialogue started shifting to, "Don't do this. Don't think that. Don't embarrass us. Be realistic. Be practical. Stop daydreaming." Basically, the message was, "It's time to get real." The message then filtered into the belief that dreams aren't real and won't get you anywhere.

Think about how a child processes that: *Okay, it must be childish to dream, and I want to be more like a grownup, so I'll stop using my imagination and stop dreaming.* Sometimes, children are even pressured to follow a specific path based on someone else's expectation or unfulfilled dream, so they contract and get stuffed into a little box, wrapped in a pretty bow. And then that child's authentic light is extinguished. Their world gets a lot smaller. Their beliefs about themselves just became external. The message they got was, *Let me look outside of myself for my truth, for my answers. Let me see what others think, and I will do what I think they think I should do.* This young child has learned to give up control of their life's design and wait for the outside world to tell them *how* to be and *who* to be. This becomes a way of thinking, a way of believing, and a way of being as they enter into adulthood.

> *"Once in a while it really hits people that they don't have to experience the world in the way they have been told."*
>
> — Alan Keightly

First and foremost, it's important to recognize we matter. Every single human on this earth matters. But it is up to each of us to believe that for ourselves. And when we do, that's when we can really lean in and feel empowered.

> *"Believe you can and you're halfway there."*
>
> — Theodore Roosevelt

The problem is we are trained to look outside ourselves for validation, when all along we already have everything we need inside us.

If you are one of those people, know what you need is waiting for you to look within to discover, realize, and become. Power flows through everyone, and you direct it.

Think of your life as a movie script. You are the writer, the director, the producer, and the star of your life movie. This book will help you get better at playing each of those roles, and so to simplify the process, the content has been split into three parts. Part I (Chapters 1-5) is where you begin to establish a foundation for your next best version. Part II (Chapters 6-12) introduces you to the Seven Step IgniteU System for Leading a Life that Lights You Up, giving you simple and effective principles to work from. Part III (Chapters 13-20) addresses breaking through the mind blocks that can stop you from moving forward and learning to reframe them in a way that has the power to propel you to new heights and align with a vision-driven life. At the end of each chapter, I've included a page to note any insights you have while reading the chapter. That insight may have ignited a thought or feeling, which I like to call an *inspired insight*. And since nothing happens until we act, I want you to follow up on each inspired insight with actions you can take to serve it, which I like to call an *inspired action*. Don't overthink this—just jot down whatever thoughts flash on the screen of your mind.

My hope is you will begin to see yourself starring in your life movie. That's right, everyone has a life script they've been rehearsing and acting out for years. Are you being and living the starring role of your life script? Do you love the script?

Remember, you matter.

You get one life. Time stops for no one. What are you waiting for?

Tear up the old script—it's been holding you back from stepping into your *what's next evolution*—and let's get this show, your show, started.

Quiet on set.

Lights.

Camera.

Action!

"It isn't where you come from. It's where you're going that counts."

— Ella Fitzgerald

PART I
ESTABLISHING A FOUNDATION

CHAPTER 1

IGNITING THE FIRE OF YOUR SOUL

"The very best thing you can do for the whole
world is to make the most of yourself."

— Wallace Wattles

The definition of ignite is to catch or cause fire; to arouse an emotion or situation; to spark or to trigger. When you seriously consider what igniting the fire of your soul means to you, think about what arouses and triggers your deepest desires. What lights you up inside, and what is seeking to emerge? This is where you want to be quiet and clear all distractions, allowing yourself to connect with your soul. Listen and be aware of your thoughts and feelings. Don't judge or dismiss any of it. Pay attention to the ideas and images revealing themselves to you. Notice what's sparking your interest and inspiring you. This is where the power of possibility is born. This is where your dreams are ignited and your purpose is fueled. What you decide to do next is crucial at this juncture.

Throughout the journey of our lives, we continually come to junctures where we must decide in which direction to move forward. That decision then reveals the next step we take, and that step will reveal the next step and so on. Each choice we make will have a set of results—good, bad, or indifferent. Now, if we're not paying attention, instead of genuinely listening to where our soul is guiding us, we will default to the world outside ourselves, which will selfishly guide us to conform to what is going on around us. And without realizing it, it will give us a false sense of self and detour us from the direction we were truly meant to go.

Listen to your soul and trust it to lead you by tapping into what matters most to you. Think about when you first set out in the world as a young adult and asked yourself, "What's next for me?" Maybe your path was not yet clear, but you were bright-eyed and full of possibilities. As you moved into your thirties and then into mid-life and the milestone fortieth and fiftieth birthdays hit, you found yourself reflecting on where you've been and what you've accomplished. Again you asked the same question, "What's next for me?"

Some find they've stopped asking what's next because they don't look at the world as being filled with possibilities anymore. Instead, the question becomes, "What's happened to me?"

More time goes by, and if you're fortunate enough to reach your golden years, you find yourself asking that question again, "What's next for me?" Transitioning into your senior years is a crucial juncture. It can be a very confusing time if you're not paying attention to your *what's next*. This is a phase many call retirement. The idea of retirement is alluring. The perception of retirement for many is stopping the daily grind of going to a job they aren't thrilled with, not having to get up early to be somewhere they really don't want to be, and not having to listen to people they'd prefer not to be around.

Unfortunately, for many of us, we get so focused on being freed from a job we don't love that we retire before clearly defining what's next. We blindly jump into this new life called retirement. At first, it's a relief. But as time marches on, we start losing our identity. Before we know it, and with no direction, we're asking ourselves, "Is this all there is? Why am I here?"

If you had kids, they gave you a purpose, but they're on their own now. They don't need you like they did before. And like it or not, your job did give you a focus, a structure, a community, and a direction, which gave you purpose. It may not have been a profound purpose or one that inspired you, but it gave you meaning nonetheless as you gave big chunks of your time and energy to it. Others were involved and you had goals. You had holiday parties, company picnics, and happy hours with colleagues.

Many people discover over time that retirement just isn't enough. Unless you've mapped out a transition strategy for yourself with the "What's next for me?" question in mind, you may find yourself settling into a *status quo* life. You're stalled like a car that's run out of gas. It's going nowhere. And until you fill up your tank with fuel to ignite your life, you'll stay in the same place, becoming stagnant and rusty.

We were not created to evolve and then retire to live out the *status quo*. We were designed to continue to grow and evolve. We do that by continuing to lean into our possibilities, by continuing to ask, "What's next for me? What's important to me? How can I serve this world using my gifts and talents? What would I love?" This is your *what's next evolution*.

> *"I say, follow your bliss and don't be afraid, and doors will open where you didn't know they were going to be."*
>
> — Joseph Campbell

I first asked myself, "What's next?" when I was a high school senior. We had to write a paper on a career we would love to pursue. I wasn't exactly clear on what that was for me. I loved fashion, clothing, and shopping. My mother and sister suggested being a personal shopper. This gave me a direction, so I went to community college with being a personal shopper in mind.

From there, I worked over the summer in the purchasing department at Macomb Community College, which I was attending. My boss always encouraged me and asked me about my career path. He gave me the idea of becoming a buyer for department stores. He had a friend who was a buyer, so he introduced me to her. I spoke with her and was hooked.

I then had a clearer path, and I was excited about it. I found a fashion merchandising program at Central Michigan University. My plan was to transfer in after completing my second year of community college.

That Christmas, I had a party at my house with many of my high school friends and classmates. At the party, a short conversation with a guy named Andy turned my plans upside down and shifted my path completely. He asked what I was doing, and when I said transferring to Central Michigan to get a degree in fashion merchandising, he said his sister did exactly that and had graduated—she was now working in accounting or something of that nature.

I was stunned. I asked him what had happened. He said, "Patti, we live in Michigan. What are you going to do with a fashion merchandising degree here?" I remember thinking he was right, and I suddenly felt sick and wanted my party to be over.

But what happened next was *key*. Instead of wallowing in the loss of my dream and giving up on my passion for fashion, I asked Andy, "What do you think I could do differently from your sister?" He said, "Why not look into a trade school for fashion? It's a niche business and connections seem important." That made perfect sense to me. I instantly decided it was exactly what I was going to do.

I only had one problem—my dad. He had worked at Chrysler and had a good position, but he could no longer move up because he did not have a college degree. He did not want that for his kids, so it was super-important to him that we all got a degree from a university.

I was so passionate and clear about my path that I (very nervously) talked to my parents. My mom was all for fashion trade school, but my dad didn't say anything at first. Finally, he said, "Well, if this is really what you would love, then I advise you to research fashion trade schools and let me know what you find."

I was off and running! I found three schools in the area, and I narrowed it down to one. I went to fashion merchandising school fully intending to become a buyer.

Then, after working hard to complete the program, a couple of months before graduation, my buying teacher asked, "What's happened? You were so passionate about this area, but that spark seems to have left you." She was so right; I just didn't want to admit it to myself. During my coursework, I realized numbers were a big part of a buyer's job. I am not passionate about numbers.

Based on the work I had done in her class, my interior design teacher told me I had a good eye and sense of style. But though I enjoyed interior design, it did not truly ignite my soul. I wasn't sure what I was going to do, but I decided to keep an open mind, which I found was key because you don't know what you don't know.

Within a week, the director of our school told us one of the hottest apparel companies at the time (it was early 1980s), *Esprit de Corp.*, was hiring at its showroom, which was not far from our school. I didn't even hear what the job was.... I just heard *Esprit* and was out the door and on my way to the showroom. I almost went home to change, but I felt a *nudge* to go straight there.

I was glad I trusted my inner voice. Another important key I learned was the power of trusting your intuition. I was first to interview, and many young women from the school showed up just after me. I was offered the job on the spot, and the position was waiting for me when I graduated. Until then, I hadn't even known what I would be doing existed. I became a manufacturer's sales representative. I sold to stores—business to business. The job included merchandising, and I presented all the season's latest fashions to buyers. That was truly it for me. It was my dream job with my dream company.

I graduated, receiving the "Most Likely to Succeed Award," and my dream job was waiting for me.

I learned so many lessons in that experience of leaning into what *ignited my soul*. Three key ones were:

1. **Pay Attention:** Listen and become aware of what truly lights you up inside, and then continue to take *inspired, imperfect action* every day toward your passion to keep you moving forward. I say inspired "imperfect" action because what often stops people from taking action is the idea of "waiting until I'm perfect at it." It's about progress, not perfection.

2. **Remain Open-Minded and Flexible:** You don't know what you don't know. Be open to pivoting, adapting, and adjusting.

3. **Stay True to What Really Matters to You:** What's most important to you at your core—what ignites your soul—is the cornerstone to everything you do and every decision you make. Trust your intuition. It's your inner pointer.

I realized when I became clear about my direction and started taking steps forward, I would continue to produce results. Things may shift and change along the way, but if you stay true to what's important to you and keep an open mind, you will continue to be passionate, grow, evolve, and be fulfilled. I also learned to trust that as one door closes, another door opens—if *I'm open* to allowing myself to see it.

"Be miserable. Or motivate yourself. Whatever
has to be done, it's always your choice."

— Wayne Dyer

You can always see things two ways. How you see things depends on the energy you decide to give them. You can have the nothing-ever-works-out attitude or the anything-is-possible attitude. One is closed and contractive, low frequency energy, and the other is an open and expansive, high frequency energy. Both are choices with results. The results can either serve you and move you forward, or keep you struggling and held back. It is all your choice. You've been given the freedom to choose your thoughts, no matter what your circumstance.

Do you choose to ignite your soul's desire for what's next for you, or do you choose to diminish your soul's desire with what's not? You actually do have the power to choose. Use your power, and don't give it away to circumstances and conditions.

As long as you are breathing, you have the power to *ignite* your passion and purpose for your what's next evolution....

"What lies behind us and what lies before us are tiny
matters compared to what lies within us."

— Ralph Waldo Emerson

Now it's time to write down the inspired insight you had from reading this chapter and then the inspired "imperfect" action you will take. Going forward, you will want to think about both as you read so you're prepared to write them down at the end of each chapter. Don't skip this exercise. It's important to take this action or your inspiration will quickly diminish.

Inspired Insight:

_____

_____

_____

_____

Inspired Action:

_____

_____

_____

_____

"A bird doesn't sing because it has an answer,

it sings because it has a song."

— Joan Walsh Anglund

CHAPTER 2

SHIFTING YOUR MINDSET TO WHAT'S POSSIBLE

"If you can change the way you look at things,
the things you look at change."

— Wayne Dyer

Your mindset is everything; it is absolutely your greatest asset. The thoughts and ideas you entertain in your mind profoundly affect how you perceive the world around you because what you believe to be true is what you actually see. The glass is half full depending on how you choose to look at it. If you want to find the positive, you will. And hanging around a group of people who believe anything is possible or your team will win more than likely will lead you to believe the same.

Positivity (like negativity) is infectious and makes all things possible. Why do you think the power of prayer is attached to miracles? Where your attention goes, energy flows. That's why what you think, you become. It's about where you decide to focus and put your energy. And it's *always* your choice. What is most important here is to have a true awareness of your thoughts and their power in taking you where you want to go.

It starts like this:

A thought comes into your mind, and you *choose* to focus on it…

Which then causes you to have feelings about that thought, giving it more energy and power…

Which causes you to act, fueled and charged by the emotion of that thought…

Which then gives you a result based on your action and the mindset that influenced it.

Whether the thought is good or bad, healthy or unhealthy, worthy or unworthy, inspiring or defeating, the fuel *you* choose to give it will determine the result you will produce. It's about aligning your thoughts and feelings with the results you want to manifest.

Understand your mindset is always your choice. Everything starts inside you. Understand that you have the power to create a life that's meaningful and fulfilling to you, but you must believe it deep in your soul. You must believe you are worthy of it and deserving of it. And believe you are also

100 percent responsible for creating it. You have the leading role in the feature film called *Your Life*.

Your life isn't out there; it's inside you waiting to be expressed and lived. No one can do it for you. You were designed to continue to grow and evolve right up to your last breath. But you were also given the power to choose your life, and it starts in your thoughts, which is where your mindset is formed every day.

"We cannot become what we want by remaining what we are."

— Max Depree

Carol Dweck, a Stanford University psychologist, wrote a very insightful book after much research called *Mindset: The New Psychology of Success*. It's about how we can *learn* to fulfill our potential. Dweck says our success relies on more than just our abilities and talent; it relies on whether we have a *fixed* or *growth* mindset when approaching goals.

A fixed mindset is the belief that you are who you are and that can't be changed. This leads to dismissing the value of effort. It also leads to an urgency to constantly try to prove yourself. A fixed mindset is always evaluating:

- Will I succeed or fail?
- Will I look smart or dumb?

- Will I be accepted or rejected?
- Will I feel like a winner or a loser?

A growth mindset believes you can continue to grow and improve through your efforts. And everyone can change and evolve through applying themselves and through their experiences. The growth mindset creates a passion for learning. And when you have a passion for stretching yourself and remaining committed, particularly when things are not going your way, it is the hallmark of the growth mindset.

"Unless you try to do something beyond what you have already mastered, you will never grow."

— Ralph Waldo Emerson

In March of 1990, I did something I never believed I could do. It required a lot of rigorous training, time, and effort. It was definitely, for me, a big stretch. And even with all the intense preparation, I would not have been able to accomplish this goal without an *aligning mindset*. It was truly a lesson in the power of the mind and its relation to achieving a big goal. I'm talking about the Los Angeles Marathon—26.4 miles, something I've never even come close to running.

I've liked running for exercise since I was young, and I was fast then. In high school, I ran sprints on the track team, but never any kind of distance. When I was twenty-five, my friend Vicki and I started running together in the mornings (5:45 a.m.) before going to the office. We worked up to three-mile runs and decided to do the 5K Pumpkin Run that fall. It was fun, and by Thanksgiving, we were running six or seven miles and feeling good.

In December, Vicki threw out an idea—what if we signed up to run the LA Marathon in March? We laughed, and I only took her half-seriously, until she called to tell me she had signed us up. I mean, it was December, and the marathon was in March, so how the heck were we going to do this?

Vicki had a friend named Val who had run some marathons and had run a few times with us. Val said we needed to start working up to running ten miles on our Saturday runs. We were already doing six- or seven-mile runs every day throughout the week, but this was a whole new level. The doubts and fears started pouring in.

Soon, Val suggested we meet on Saturday for a ten-mile run. It was great having a mentor to help us structure working up to our goal, someone who had already accomplished this big feat. It was a push, but we did it. We continued, eventually moving to twelve miles. We kept plodding forward until the big test came.

Val said preparing mentally was just as important as being physically prepared for the marathon. What that meant for us was running eighteen miles two weeks prior to the marathon at least once, so mentally, we knew we could do twenty-six. The idea being if you can run eighteen miles, you can run twenty-six miles. Val told Vicki and me that she would run with us for moral support. We committed to a day and time. Well, wouldn't you know it, that day I had an emergency at work that delayed me. I was coming from downtown Los Angeles (this was before cell phones), so I was late meeting Val and Vicki. When I didn't arrive, they took off.

"If you aren't going all the way, why go at all?"

— Joe Namath

I was at a fork in the road. I knew this was my test. I could go home and hope I could find time in the next day or two to run eighteen miles, or I could just not do it. I knew I had to know for myself mentally that I could do it, so I parked my car and set off, running on my own. The doubts started pouring in. Vicki and I always had each other to push the other through, but how would I do it on my own? At first, my mindset was that I really didn't think I could do it. It was already getting late, and I really didn't know if I could push through on my own. At one point, I was running uphill when an older woman who was walking downhill yelled to me to run faster. I wanted to scream, but I just kept running.

It's amazing how your mind can start working for you. This awareness was huge in understanding the importance of being committed, clear, and focused on your goal. At one point, I began solely concentrating on the ice-cold Gatorade I had waiting for me in the fridge. With as much persistence as I could muster, I finally finished the entire eighteen-mile run!

As I walked to my car, I felt an incredible shift—now I truly believed I could run and finish a marathon. And better yet, I had done it on my own. All the effort and training had paid off. This achievement came with some added bonuses. One was training on the big hills in the Los Feliz area where Vicki lived, and another was that her home was directly on my way to work, which made it convenient for early morning training. Some days, we ran up to the infamous Greek Theatre where we often encountered coyotes. On other days, when we didn't have time for a longer run, we conquered the hill we called "Heart-Attack Hill"—a big hill we zig-zagged up and down. We always made our challenging runs an adventure.

Marathon day came. The hills we confronted were small compared to the hills we had trained in. I can't quite explain the emotions that poured over me when I crossed the finish line. I couldn't believe I had actually completed a full marathon—in four hours and forty-one minutes. It was such an awesome feat! One that down the road paid off in ways I couldn't have imagined.

Completing the LA Marathon was yet more evidence, along with landing my dream job, of the value of aligning goals with mindset. And evidence that the final piece to achieving success is putting in the effort required to cross the finish line.

> *"Without self-discipline success is impossible, period."*
>
> — Lou Holtz

Fast forward a few years—I was interviewing for a position at an up-and-coming apparel company called Rampage. I had never interviewed with so many managers before. I eventually ended up sitting down with the CEO and founder.

He walked in the room reading my resume and then looked up at me. He made one comment. "I see here you ran the LA Marathon. I know the discipline, focus, and effort this took both mentally and physically. I don't need to know much more. You're hired." I never imagined running a marathon could directly affect an incredible job opportunity in the fashion business. What a lesson in how cultivating an anything-is-possible mindset can truly make anything possible—even when we can't imagine it. Mindset absolutely matters and affects everything.

> *"A lot of conflict you have in your life exists simply because you're not living in alignment; you're not being true to yourself."*
>
> — Steve Maraboli

Kobe Bryant was a great example of someone who adopted and aligned with a growth mindset early in life. In an interview, he said his parents instilled in him the importance of imagination and curiosity when he was young. They taught him that if you want to accomplish something, you can, but you have to put in the work. He said he grew up thinking the world was his oyster. He grew up with the fundamental belief that anything is possible if you're willing to put in the work, effort, and sacrifice.

Bryant told a story about going to a summer basketball camp when he was eleven. He did not score a point all summer, not one shot or free throw went in. The first thing he did was work on shooting every day. He got better. And by the time he was fourteen, he was killing it.

"Hard work beats talent when talent doesn't work hard."

— Tim Notke

What Bryant learned was he had to work on the fundamentals. He had to get those down first and do them well. Because he stuck to the fundamentals, he caught up to the other players. He eventually grew, and with the fundamentals down, an eagerness to do the hard work, and a positive mindset, plus his newfound athleticism, he, at fourteen, earned Best in State. He said if you play every day for two to three hours, just think about how much better you'll get. He summed it up by saying, "Show up every single day and do the work."

"You have to expect things of yourself before you can do them."

— Michael Jordan

Bryant learned how to leverage a key advantage over his competition—to outwork everyone. And his discipline and work ethic didn't change when he became a professional. He woke up at 4 a.m. every day and was always the first to show up for practice and the last to leave. He became known for his focus mentality. This eventually became what Bryant called mamba mentality, which is a constant quest to be better today than you were yesterday. It's about trying to be the best version of yourself. It's a way of life. Now that's a growth mindset, one of limitless possibility, heart, passion, and the willingness to do whatever it takes.

"Success is no accident. It is hard work, perseverance, learning, studying, sacrifice, and most of all, love of what you are doing or learning to do."

— Pele

Stan Beecham is a sports psychologist and the author of *Elite Minds: How Winners Think Differently to Create a Competitive Edge and Maximize Success.* In a *Forbes* interview, he talked about how the primary factor in success isn't talent or experience; it's mindset. He discussed how important the mental game is in sports and business and how the mind controls the body. He suggests thinking of your brain as the computer and your beliefs as the software.

What you think dictates what you become, just as the software dictates how your computer operates. Your subconscious (where your beliefs live) doesn't know the difference between what's real and what's not. It just takes in the information it is fed as truth, which becomes your beliefs, and it produces behavior that aligns with that truth. It's super-important to be aware of what you're telling yourself.

What beliefs are you programming into your subconscious? What you actually believe about yourself and for yourself is the program that will drive you toward what you believe to be true. When you believe in yourself and in your potential, and then forge ahead expecting to do well, you will. Your focus is on doing your job to the best of your ability or playing your sport better or acting out your role better—it's about stretching yourself to your next best version. Focus on what you want, not what you don't want.

I realize I've used a lot of sports examples, including my own in this chapter on working with mindset. Because the mind-body connection is strongly connected with developing as an athlete, I think such examples provide a simple way of examining the connection between the subconscious and personal development.

That said, I'd like to tell you about my grandmother on my dad's side, and how, at ninety, her laser-focused mindset made what seemed impossible, possible.

My grandmother Anna was not an athlete. She didn't watch sports or attend many of her son's high school football games. She was a tough woman who came to America from Ukraine by herself at sixteen. She did not speak English. Anna weathered the Great Depression while raising three children, and unfortunately, was widowed in her early forties. She was scared but had already adopted a survivor mindset through her life experiences. She always had a good attitude and was grateful for everything. When she didn't understand something, she just laughed.

When Anna was in her early nineties, she slipped on a rug in her basement and broke her hip. She couldn't walk and didn't have a phone in the basement. (This was the mid-1990s when cell phones weren't so popular). Laser-focused on getting help and coming from a "What *can* I do?" mindset, with a broken hip and a stout frame, she patiently pulled herself up the basement steps, one at a time. From there, Anna dragged herself across the kitchen floor, through the living room, and down to the end of the hall to the phone and called my dad. (Why that was her only phone, I don't know.) Then she dragged herself back through the hallway, living room, and kitchen, and pulled herself up to unlatch the door. She waited for my dad to take her to the hospital. Anna came through quite remarkably, considering at her age a broken hip is typically the beginning of the end.

Of course, immediately after, she had a phone installed in the basement and kitchen. (Hallelujah!) What an example of mind over matter, despite age or condition.

Mindset is key and always your choice. It can get you through or take you down. The power of the mind is beyond comprehension, and the power of possibility is limitless. But you hold that power in how you choose to think. The glass is half full if you see it that way.

"I've learned from experience that the greater part of our happiness or misery depends on our dispositions and not on our circumstances."

— Martha Washington

Inspired Insight:

_____

_____

_____

_____

Inspired Action:

_____

_____

_____

_____

"Human beings can alter their lives by altering their attitudes of mind."

— William James

?

CHAPTER 3

LETTING GO TO MOVE FORWARD

"Give your stress wings and let it fly away."

— Terri Guillemets

Letting go of something, someone, some thought, or even some way of thinking can be one of the most difficult things to do. Yet it is one of the most empowering ways to actually move ourselves forward. Why is that?

For one thing, we only have so much time in each day. We only have so much room in our mind. We have twenty-four hours in a day, and we fill that time with activities—everyone gets the same number of hours each day. The only difference between people is how they choose to use their twenty-four hours. We all choose what we pay attention to, whom we spend time with, what we read, what we eat, how we choose to exercise and move, and what we choose to think about and align with. And part of that process is evaluating which thoughts, actions, and people serve our growth and which need to be released.

Focus in on an area where you want a different result, an area you want to improve. Start with a simple assessment of the current situation; then look at your behavior in that area. How do you spend your time? Who are you surrounded by? Do they align with your goals? Look at your own thoughts and actions. Are they aligned with the result you would love?

Is some situation, thought, action, or person that was once in harmony with your vision of what's next, now no longer aligned with how you would love to move forward? This is an important juncture. You have a choice to bless and release someone, something, some group, or even a thought that isn't on the same frequency as you and your dream anymore. It is critical to let go here to make room for the people, opportunities, and ideas that will help you evolve and move toward where you want to go. This is where you align harmoniously with what you would love. But you must make room for it. And the only way to do that is to let go and release what isn't serving your vision, allowing space for what is aligned with the result you would love.

"Some people believe holding on and hanging in there are signs of great strength. However, there are times when it takes much more strength to know when to let go and then do it."

— Alyson Lander

Shortly after I moved to California, I met a great guy with whom I had an instant deep connection. The connection continued to grow as time went on. We had great conversations and great chemistry. But looking back, what we each wanted from a relationship was not aligned. I deeply desired a committed relationship. I also wanted to get married and have a family at some point, though at the time I was primarily focused on my career. His desires were different. He enjoyed dating and didn't really want to get married. He was upfront about it. I respected that and figured it was okay at that point since I was focused on my fashion career and traveled around the country frequently.

We had fun together and continued to date other people and each other. But it became clear I was developing a deeper connection to him. I pushed it down for a while, realizing our desires weren't aligned. But I couldn't deny my feelings. Commuting downtown meant being in the car for an hour each way every day. I listened to music and sometimes imagined walking down the aisle with him. It felt so natural and even made me tear up at times. I chalked it up to a beautiful daydream.

We dated on these terms for ten years!

I got to the point where I was down on my knees praying to God to please just put out the flame in my heart if it were not meant to be. I loved this man deeply, but if we weren't meant to be (aligned), I just wanted so badly to be over him once and for all. But the flame didn't flicker; it just grew.

Eventually, after about eight years, we began dating exclusively. Two years into that, our relationship went like this—we'd have a conversation in which he would say he just wasn't ready for anything more than where we were, and he was happy with the way things were. He was comfortable. I finally reached a place in my heart where I knew if I didn't do something different, I would be on this gerbil wheel for another year, or two, or three. Although I couldn't deny the love and connection we had, I also couldn't deny I was starting to feel resentment.

In that moment of realization, I knew it was time. I didn't want to regret the relationship we had built because we really did have a good run, so I told myself I needed to release it. Knowing that was the next best move for me was one thing, but actually going through with it was very scary and uncomfortable. It had been ten years and a lot of emotional investment.

On the Friday of Labor Day weekend, I was still at work. I knew it was time. I needed to have the talk that weekend. I had stopped discussing my relationship with my friends and family since they thought I was wasting my time with someone who was a great guy but would never commit.

Without overthinking it, I told my designer Susan, who knew our story, that I was going to have the talk, knowing it would likely result in our breaking up for good. Fast forward to late Monday afternoon. I'd had a pit in my stomach all weekend and just couldn't bring myself to talk to him about it. It was eating me up inside. I truly believe if I had not told Susan I was going to do it once and for all, I wouldn't have done it.

I went back and forth in my head until the weekend was almost over. I didn't know if I was ready to let go. Finally, the thought of telling Susan I couldn't do it was too much. I didn't realize at the time that telling her had helped hold me accountable, which pushed me to start the uncomfortable conversation I'd been avoiding all weekend. And just like that, it was over. Most of me knew he wasn't going to say yes…let's do this thing—let's get married. But there was still that tiny part of me that had been hoping he would.

This was absolutely a pivotal point in my life. I left his house feeling relieved to have done what I knew I needed to do because I was clear about why I needed to do it. But other than some brief relief, what hit me like a freight train was a deluge of mixed emotions, sadness, and emptiness. I drove back to my apartment, laid in bed, and cried my eyes out. I was absolutely devasted and heartbroken. I remember feeling numb for days and weeks.

By October, I was getting by okay and really focused on my work. I remember the day I fully released the relationship for good. It was at an event our company put on at the train station in downtown Los Angeles. I was on the dance floor when the song came on. A woman from our New York office was there. She was just coming off a broken engagement. We both needed the release and started singing along at the top of our lungs—we sang every word of "I Will Survive!" by Gloria Gaynor as we danced our hearts out.

I left all the sadness and emptiness I was carrying inside on the dance floor. The next morning, I felt a lightness. I knew in that moment I was finally ready to move on. I felt such release. It had been a beautiful chapter, but it needed to end to make room for the relationship I deeply desired, one that aligned with what I was finally ready to welcome.

> *"Letting go isn't about having the courage to release the past;*
> *it's about having the wisdom to embrace the present."*
>
> — Steve Maraboli

I never could have imagined what happened next. I had blessed and released my relationship with the guy I thought was the love of my life. I was finally ready to move on, date, and evolve. I could fill another chapter with what happened next, but let's just say as I made room for the relationship I deeply desired, releasing the one that wasn't working for me anymore, my world changed. By the end of the following year, I was engaged to a man who was completely aligned with me. Interestingly enough, it turned out to be the same guy I released on the dance floor at the train station! Life is truly full of beautiful surprises if we just make room for what we would love more of and release what doesn't serve our vision. And as I learned, even if it is ultimately what's meant to be, still you must first release what isn't serving your vision and what's not aligned with it to make room for the version that is.

"Let go of the past, but keep the lessons it taught you."

— Chiara Gizzi

One of the most significant aspects of truly understanding letting go is forgiveness. Some awful things go on out there that seem unforgivable. Abuse, torture, cruelty, deception…all despicable acts, and yet the ability to forgive these things can truly set you free when you understand what forgiveness truly is and means.

Forgiveness is not about letting someone off the hook for a bad deed. Nor is it a bargaining chip to hold someone emotionally hostage for doing wrong. Forgiveness isn't for the other person who has crossed the line; forgiveness is for you. It's about letting go of what happened so it can't hold you hostage and keep you from moving forward. And it's also important to forgive yourself when you did something you might not be so proud of.

When you look at forgiveness as a practice in letting go of toxicity and negativity, it takes on a whole new meaning. Hanging onto anger, angst, bitterness, regret, shame, or judgment absolutely does not serve you. In fact, it blocks you. It is toxic. Toxicity debilitates and kills. It's like drinking poison. And the longer you hold onto it, the more damage it does. As difficult as it can be, forgiveness is such a freeing process.

"True forgiveness is one of the most healing, releasing,
and freeing gifts we give to ourselves."

— Brandon Bays

When my older sister Marie passed away, I faced the Mt. Everest of challenges in letting go and forgiveness. Marie had gone through a bitter divorce some years prior with much angst that continued up until her death. Consequently, lots of bad blood existed between her ex and our family. At first, we did not want him to attend the funeral. The afternoon before the funeral service, my mom, younger sister, and I were at the church talking to the priest, Father McNamara (Father Mac), about the service.

My stomach had been unsettled all day. It bothered me so much that, as we walked out of the church with the priest, without even thinking, I found myself pouring this dilemma out to him. Marie's children, who were eleven and fourteen at the time, would be there. They had just lost their mother. But many of us really didn't want to see their father. What bothered me most was I really didn't believe Marie would have wanted him there, and that was weighing heavily on me. I wanted to honor Marie's wishes, yet I felt very conflicted.

What Father Mac said was pivotal. He asked, "Do you believe your sister is in a better place? Do you believe she's not suffering anymore? Do you believe she's at peace?"

I answered, "Yes, I believe she's in a better place. I don't believe she's suffering anymore. I believe she's at peace."

"Coming from that place," Father Mac replied, "what do you think she would want?"

And in that instant, I knew exactly what we had to do. I told my mom and sister Marie's ex had to be invited, and I was going to call him as soon as we got home. I realized Marie's kids would be attending their mom's funeral, and they absolutely needed their remaining parent there with them.

It wasn't an easy call, but I told Marie's ex exactly what had just happened—every bit of the conversation with Father Mac and what I was thinking. He was surprised to hear from me, but thankful. We agreed to put our ill feelings aside and move forward in the best interest of the kids.

The funeral ceremony was emotional and healing. Father Mac helped me see past the hurt, and it changed the entire dynamic of the day. It actually brought families together for the greater good and brought peace back into our lives.

After the funeral, we invited Marie's ex to come to our home for the funeral luncheon. Some people were shocked to see him, and though it wasn't easy for any of us, including him, it truly was freeing to let go of all the anger.

When I let go, it allowed me to see what was most important—those kids needed their parent that day.

What I learned was when we don't allow ourselves to forgive, we essentially put ourselves in an emotional prison. Putting up walls keeps us from truly moving forward. Where we place our attention is where our energy goes. Life is precious, and so is time. Bless, release, and move forward.

"Releasing the burdens from the past allows your soul to take the next step forward without limitations."

— Matt Fraser

In the late 1990s, I came across the book *The Art of Happiness* by the Dalai Lama. I really enjoyed its content and message. I was also struck by Buddhist culture and the importance it places on learning to live from compassion no matter what. The Dalai Lama talks about cultivating compassion by being empathetic toward others and actively being open to seeing things from their perspective. In doing so, you cultivate universal compassion toward your fellow humans, which is the path to a healthier, happier life. What a beautiful concept and deep foundation to build your life on—pure compassion for your fellow human. It is a simple concept, but it is not easy to do and do consistently throughout our lives.

More recently, I saw a YouTube video of a talk the Dalai Lama gave on *The Power of Forgiveness* at the University of Limerick in Ireland. He told a story of a Buddhist monk he knew who had been imprisoned by the Communist Chinese government for eighteen years. When the Dalai Lama finally saw him, he asked him about his experience. The monk told the Dalai Lama he had been in real danger a few times. Thinking that meant physical danger, the Dalai Lama asked him to explain. The monk said he had almost lost compassion a few times.

"Compassion is the basis of morality."

— Arthur Schopenhauer

What an evolved level of awareness! And this was while living for years in terrible circumstances and awful conditions, enduring cruel behavior yet holding and maintaining a vibration of pure compassion for the very people who mistreated him. What a living, breathing example of pure compassion for your fellow human.

"Compassion and tolerance are not a sign of weakness, but a sign of strength."

— Dalai Lama

Compassion is the epitome of getting out of your ego to open up and allow yourself to look past human behavior and into the soul of the individual. Looking past human behavior is the Mt. Everest for each of us. In *A Course in Miracles*, it says, "Every act is either an expression of love or a call for love, regardless of how unskillful it may seem." One of my mentors, Mary Morrissey, said something that really helped me let go of negative human behavior directed at me. She called it "unskilled behavior that can be blessed and released." That was an aha moment for me. When I adopted that perspective, it helped me instantly release ill feelings and frustration. And this practice can be applied to seemingly insignificant situations that nonetheless still get your blood pressure up.

"One can overcome the forces of negative emotions, like anger and hatred, by cultivating their counter forces, like love and compassion."

— Dalai Lama

I distinctly remember the day I put this way of being into practice. I was pulling out of a parking spot when a car cut me off. I slammed on my brakes, barely avoiding getting hit. Once I pulled out and was heading toward the exit, that same car cut me off again. For a second, my reaction was to shout out something and lay on my horn.

Instead, I hit my mental pause button, then simply blessed and released the unskilled behavior. And just like that, the animosity went away.

When I got home, I realized how it could have gone: I honk the horn, yell loudly, get worked up, and then bring that energy home with me. Then my family and dogs would get to experience the remnants of my angst. And all because someone cut me off. I found it truly remarkable how quickly my angst dissipated when I chalked it up as unskilled behavior and let it go. It was so liberating that I adopted this technique as a new way of being, a new behavior. Am I perfect at it? No. But since I have adopted a new awareness that serves me better, I quickly do an autocorrect. When I catch myself reacting and hanging on to someone else's unskilled behavior, or even my own for that matter, I remember to pause, bless, and release. It's freeing.

"There is a nobility in compassion, a beauty in empathy, a grace in forgiveness."

— John Connolly

Inspired Insight:

_____

_____

_____

_____

Inspired Action:

_____

_____

_____

_____

"Holding on is believing that there's only a past;

letting go is knowing that there's a future."

— Daphne Rose Kingma

CHAPTER 4

LEADING YOUR LIFE

*"We all have to start with ourselves. It is time to walk the
talk. Take the journey of making very difficult decisions. Start
removing things from your life that are not filling your cup
and adding things that bring joy into your life."*

— Lisa Hammond

What does it mean to be a leader? It means being someone
who takes charge and is strong, bold, visionary, courageous,
responsible, accountable, inspiring, and difference-
making. My question is: Do you see yourself as a leader? Some already
call themselves leaders because they've taken on a leadership role. We
typically identify with leaders in government and business, for example.
But what about being the leader of your own life? Who better to lead your
life than you? Yet how many people really see themselves as true leaders?

"Take the responsibility of your own happiness;
never put it in other people's hands."

— Roy T. Bennett

One of my favorite holiday movies is *The Holiday.* Kate Winslet's character Iris, who lives in England, does a house exchange over the holidays with Cameron Diaz's character Amanda, who lives in Los Angeles. Iris is getting away to deal with a bad relationship, and Amanda is dealing with a breakup. Iris befriends an elderly man named Arthur, who, to her surprise, is an Oscar-winning screenwriter. While they're at dinner, Arthur asks Iris why a beautiful woman like her would go to a stranger's house for Christmas vacation and then spend a Saturday night with an old guy like him. Iris explains she's getting away from an ex-boyfriend who broke her heart and has been stringing her along, even though he has recently gotten engaged. Arthur comments, "In the movies we have leading ladies, and we have the best friend. You, I can tell, are a leading lady, but for some reason you're behaving like the best friend." Iris replies, "You're so right. You're supposed to be the leading lady of your own life, for God's sake!"

I love that line. What a great awareness.

I have to admit I didn't feel like the leading lady earlier in my own life. As the middle child of six, one of the roles I took on was the peacemaker. I always wanted everyone to get along, so I often went along with most of my siblings' ideas, being more focused on people pleasing. This didn't help much in developing my decision-making ability, which is paramount to a leader. I didn't yet appreciate the value of deciding things for myself. Growing up, I really looked up to my older sister Marie and counted on her advice. I often went to her to ask, "What should I do?" My mom was my other advisor, and I came to her with the same question. When I was a teen, both my sister and mother started holding me accountable, making me answer that question myself. They told me I needed to start deciding things for myself. It was uncomfortable and difficult at first because that familiar little voice would challenge me by asking, "What if you make the wrong decision?"

> "Every decision brings with it some good, some bad, some lessons, and some luck. The only thing that's for sure is that indecision steals many years from many people who wind up wishing they'd just had the courage to leap."
>
> — Doe Zantamata

I was more focused on failing and what other people would think of me if I did than on figuring out what I should do to serve my growth, my what's next? Indecision is really fear-based and only takes away your power to choose for yourself.

I am so thankful to both my mom and sister for holding their ground with me, keeping me accountable, and instilling the value of deciding for myself. It pushed me to spread my own wings and learn to trust myself to make my own decisions. It helped me build not only my confidence muscle but the beginnings of my leadership muscle as the director of my own life.

My husband Tommy takes the idea of really owning everything that happens in our lives to the next level. His stance starts with a grounding in gratitude. He always says, "Look at our lives right now. We're so fortunate, and we need to remind ourselves of that every day." He's very compassionate when it comes to people who work hard in difficult situations or who have disabilities, but has no patience for complainers. Forget having a bad day around him. He'd say if you're not happy, either do something about it or accept it and move on. Life is too short, and his perspective is if you're not part of the solution, you're part of the problem.

Tommy is such a profound example of someone who took complete responsibility for his life and his choices. If something beyond his control happens and has a negative consequence for him, he says it was his fault, meaning his responsibility. At first, I'd argue it wasn't his fault, but later I realized he looked at it as a leader who takes responsibility whether he made a poor choice or just had bad luck. And owning everything that happened carried forward into his decision making.

When I asked him how he maintained the confidence to make difficult decisions when things got challenging and everything was on the line, he explained he makes the best decision he can at the time with the information he has, even with little to go on. But it is better to decide. And if it turns out the decision wasn't good, he just makes a new decision and moves on.

> *"It doesn't matter which side of the fence you get off on sometimes. What matters most is getting off. You cannot make progress without making decisions."*
>
> — Jim Rohn

Decisiveness is what actually effects change and moves us forward on our what's next journey. We'll always be faced with decisions. It's a big part of leadership, which starts with how we lead ourselves. From that, we set the example for those around us. Now think about a leader as a role model. We lead by the example we live out every day. The words we use, the actions we take, the decisions we make, and how we handle mistakes and failures set an example. Our kids are watching us as parents, as older siblings, as teachers, as coaches, as government and community officials, as business owners, as bosses, as athletes, as entertainers—as adults and role models who have influence. How are we leading by example? It's good to check in with ourselves every so often.

"Leaders must live by the same principles and values that they expect from their teams and people. Leadership is about action: leaders must do their part before asking others to do theirs. Walk the walk; don't just talk."

— Brian Hiner

I was truly inspired watching a seven-year-old connect with her inner leader as she made a decision and courageously demonstrated positive assertiveness by standing up for herself, which is another part of being a leader. This seven-year-old was my daughter Christina. It was her first day in first grade. She was looking forward to finding out which class she would be assigned to and was hoping she'd have some friends from kindergarten in her class—happily, she did.

Later that morning, we found out my older sister Marie, who had been battling cancer off and on for eight years, had received a terminal diagnosis. We were stunned!

Marie was divorced and shared custody of her two children, one in middle school and the other just starting high school. When we learned of this new prognosis, we all decided it was best to move Marie into our home full-time and her kids part-time since she shared custody with her ex-husband. That meant we would have three children going to three different schools at our house every other week. Marie was just starting chemo treatments to extend her eight-weeks-to-live prognosis. Needless to say, it was a tidal wave of change and uncertainty.

When I picked Christina up from school, she told me they had pulled her out of her classroom and put her in a split-class. That meant half the kids were first graders and the other half were second graders. At first Christina seemed okay with that situation, but the next day, she realized she didn't know anyone in the new class and half the kids were a grade older. She was upset and didn't want to go to school. I thought, *I just can't deal with this right now…. Our family can't handle this right now.* I knew Christina needed some stability since so much was going on at home.

> "*A leader takes people where they want to go. A great leader takes people where they don't necessarily want to go, but ought to be.*"
>
> — Rosalynn Carter

Christina asked if I could talk to the teacher, so I did. I explained what was happening at home, and the teacher recommended I speak with the principal, so I did. Through shared tears and a box of Kleenex, the principal, to my surprise, said she understood my position, but she and Christina's teacher believed Christina should be in an accelerated learning environment. I told her I didn't think it was a good idea because of what was going on in our family. She asked me to give it some time to see. I walked out of the school shell-shocked, but I was so out of sorts with everything going on I thought, *Okay, we'll see what happens.*

When I picked up Christina from school that day, in her little voice she said, "So what did the principal say, Mommy?" I told her what the principal said about trying it and that the principal had offered to speak to her about it if she ever wanted to. Surprisingly, Christina's immediate response was, "I want to speak to the principal. Can you set up a meeting tomorrow?" I said if she did this, it would be *her* meeting. Again, she quickly said, "That's fine." So, I scheduled the meeting, knowing full well Christina might not speak at all.

What happened when we walked into the principal's office and sat down was truly remarkable to watch. Christina didn't sit there speechless. This kid let it rip! She vehemently said the situation was uncomfortable and made her sad. She expressed how badly she wanted to be with her friends. Christina added she was very upset with the outcome of my meeting with the principal.

Watching the exchange, it was refreshing to see the principal demonstrate great leadership skills by listening closely while making engaging eye contact with Christina. The principal gave Christina room to vent and allowed her to speak her mind. The principal assured Christina she understood she was upset. Then the principal explained why she thought Christina was a perfect fit for the split classroom and asked if she would give it try. If it didn't go well, Christina could go back to her other classroom.

The principal showed this youngster proper respect by having a meeting with her, listening intently and with compassion, and giving Christina the platform to speak her mind. And afterward, the principal acknowledged Christina's strengths and explained she wanted to help Christina grow into the best version of herself. What a beautiful modeling of true leadership!

Christina said, "Okay," and we walked out. And as we left the school, she looked at me and said, "You know what, Mommy? I'm okay now. I don't need to change into the other classroom." And just like that, she moved on and forward. It was truly inspiring to watch my child stand up and bravely, confidently assert herself. She was not afraid to respectfully challenge an authority figure.

The principal offered an amazing learning and growth opportunity, giving Christina the respect the principal herself asks for from students and faculty every day. She walked her talk. What a great example.

"The most basic of all human needs is the need to understand and be understood. The best way to understand people is to listen to them."

— Ralph Nichols

Christina soon made a new friend in the split classroom and continued to adapt within a challenging environment, both in school and at home.

The teacher told me one day Christina raised her hand and went on to explain to the entire class what was going on with her Aunt Marie and how sad it made her. The teacher told me she herself had to hold back the tears, but she was inspired by Christina's courage and ability to be vulnerable and express herself. Christina demonstrated the beginnings of leading from within—stepping into her inner leader and finding her voice in her own vulnerability.

> *"When you find the courage to use your voice, it has the power to positively inspire and change the lives of others. It's one of the special gifts you have to offer the world and is something to be cherished and championed, never hidden."*
>
> — Nicole O'Neill

My dad worked hard to provide for our family, and I believe he saw himself as a leader in that role. My mom worked hard raising a big family, but I don't think she saw herself as a leader. What a mother does daily requires so many leadership qualities—especially when you're raising six children.

Being a mom is like running a small company. Mom had a small budget to work with, and that was all, period. She went without new clothes or shoes for years. She learned to sew so her kids sometimes got a new outfit, since most of our clothes were hand-me-downs. All six of us were in a Ukrainian dance group. Being on a tight budget, Mom made our costumes by hand. When we went anywhere, she "herded us like a shepherd," ensuring we were all ready before she hastily finished getting ready herself.

When my sister Carrie, the youngest, was finally in school, Mom wanted to go back to work part time. She hadn't worked since having her first child. Dad didn't want her to go to work because he couldn't see how the family would function if she did. Watching her stand up for herself was quite inspiring. Her burning desire was to do something for herself, and she was focused on going back to work part time. What happened next was truly awesome.

"Actions prove who someone is; words just prove who they want to be."

— Anthon St. Maarten

One Sunday when we were all at church, a man from the parish who knew our family came up to Mom and said he had heard through the grapevine she was looking for part-time work. When she said that was correct, he offered her a job right on the spot. He owned a small insurance company and was looking for someone to help in the office. She was taken aback—no interview, no resume?

He said for many years he'd seen our family at church on time every

Sunday. He said the six of us were always put together and well behaved. He said if Mom could do that, she could run his small office. The leadership she had demonstrated with our family hadn't gone unnoticed.

That was a new beginning for Mom as she continued to lead her family and herself into her what's next evolution. Hats off to all the moms and single parents out there managing their families as their own little enterprise. I hope you see yourself as the leader you are. I think that brave move made my mom a better mother because she led her children by leading herself.

"Instruction is good for a child; but example is worth more."

— Alexandre Dumas

When you turn within, connect with what's important to you, and allow your inner voice to be expressed, it's amazing how liberating it can be. We have this incredible opportunity to be leaders of our own life and be difference makers. We were all created with special gifts and talents. Those gifts were given to us to be expressed in the world. And these incredible gifts are the very thing that ignites our soul and seeds our purpose as we connect with our inner leader.

Our journey is to continue to evolve through discovering our passions and then taking inspired action every day toward those aspirations that feed our spirit. That's what following our dreams is really about. It's about discovery. It's about getting to know our authentic self, getting to know the very things that make us come alive. This is where we begin, our very core.

"A great leader's courage to fulfill their vision
comes from passion, not position."

— John Maxwell

Bringing out your inner leader takes courage. Courage moves you to action despite being in the center of fear. Having courage is the secret to moving through trepidation to trying new things. Sandra Yancey, CEO of eWomen Network, said something that has really stuck with me: "Courage comes before confidence." That makes total sense because confidence is an outcome. It's a result of having the courage to jump into action by attempting something new. Once you try, you realize whatever it was is not as scary as you imagined, which then emboldens you to do that thing again. And through practice and constant effort, you hone your skills and master what was once unknown. The outcome is newfound confidence. Let your dreams and your passions lead you.

"You are not here merely to make a living. You are here in order
to enable the world to live more amply, with greater vision, with
a finer spirit of hope and achievement. You are here to enrich
the world, and you impoverish yourself if you forget the errand."

— Woodrow Wilson

Being a leader means fulfillment rarely comes from others. Your life is driven by what matters most to you. You have the lead role in your life. It's time to step into your spotlight. Your dreams help you evolve and inspire those around you to do the same. Leaders are trail blazers. When you have the courage to really go for something, a path that fills you up and has deep meaning, you are a trail blazer, and you will inspire others to leave the world a better place than they found it.

"Before you are a leader, success is all about growing yourself. When you become a leader, success is all about growing others."

— Jack Welch

Inspired Insight:

_____

_____

_____

_____

Inspired Action:

Write down the ways you would love to be a leader in your life.

_____

_____

_____

_____

"How we lead ourselves in life impacts how we lead those around us."

— Michael Hyatt

CHAPTER 5

CONNECTING WITH YOUR WHY

"Definiteness of purpose is the starting point of all achievement."

— W. Clement Stone

When I first saw Simon Sinek's TedTalk about his book, *Start with Why—How Great Leaders Inspire Everyone to Take Action*, his message instantly resonated with me. He spoke of how some companies truly connect with their customers by leading with their company mission and core beliefs instead of attempting to connect by highlighting their product's attributes. Sinek concluded, "People don't buy *what* you do; they buy *why* you do it. And what you do serves as proof of what you believe."

To back up this point, Sinek uses the example of Martin Luther King, Jr.

inspiring 250,000 people to march on Washington, DC, through word of mouth. This enormous crowd gathered not so much to see King speak. They came because its members' beliefs aligned with what King believed—that all people could be treated as equals regardless of their race. Sinek calls it your why, which is essentially your core beliefs about what's most important to you, what you deeply value.

"The heart of human excellence often begins when you discover a pursuit that absorbs you, frees you, challenges you, or gives you a sense of meaning, joy, or passion."

— Terry Orliek

Your why is also the best place to start in discovering your what's next. Start with what really matters to you. That is where passion and purpose sync up. It's about embracing deep desire with intention to make a difference. Your why is who you are at your core. It's the common yarn that weaves through your life and brings out the best version of you, providing inspiration and fulfillment.

Think about a time when you really pursued something that had deep meaning. Think about experiences or people who inspired you and why.

We all have stories with a common thread attached to the truth of who we are at our core. And it is for us to *discover* that truth and express it in the world.

"Who looks outside, dreams. Who looks inside, awakens."

— Carl Gustav Jung

Here is my why story: I grew up in Michigan, a middle child of six, three boys and three girls. My mom loved to read and encouraged all her children to do so. Consequently, my three older siblings became avid readers. And me, well, I liked picture books that aroused my imagination. I loved fashion. And I thought something was wrong with me because I wasn't that into the Hardy Boys and Nancy Drew like my older siblings.

I tried to like reading, but I just didn't—or so I thought until I discovered fashion magazines. My favorite was *Cosmopolitan* since it included not only fashion but what I later came to realize were personal development articles. In fact, I still have the folder my mom saved and gave me years later with many of the self-help articles I had torn out.

Growing up, my family called me Florence Nightingale because I was constantly on the phone with friends, helping them with their problems, or rushing out the door to go console them. When my family teased me about this, I passionately told them helping people is the most important thing a person can do. Looking back, my pull toward helping people, personal growth, connection, relationships, and inspiring individuals to step into the very best version of themselves was a big part of my core values.

I find it humorous that fashion and personal development—the two things that influenced me most—to follow my profound dream of finding meaningful work I loved, came from reading *Cosmo*. Fashion inspired me to dream about working in the apparel industry and traveling to New York City. I also loved the mountains and dreamed of living out west. I did that, building a successful career in the apparel industry while living in Los Angeles and traveling to New York City eight to nine times a year for most of my twenties and thirties. I loved my life and enjoyed helping buyers put together beautiful clothing collections to serve their customers' needs and build strong relationships with them. It was always about the people for me.

As for personal development, spending chunks of time on planes from the West Coast to the East Coast gave me a lot of downtime for reading, something I looked forward to and enjoyed by that time. My interests opened up, and I discovered *INC. Magazine* and *Working Woman*. I realized I loved fashion *and* had a deep fascination for learning about entrepreneurs, women CEOs, and building something meaningful. I found myself immersed in self-help articles on topics from business to relationships. I started buying self-help books, yes actual books, on selling and marketing on a shoestring budget. I read Harvey Mackey's *Swim with the Sharks Without Being Eaten Alive*, Jack Canfield's *Success Principles*, and the Dalai Lama's *The Art of Happiness*. I even invested in my first cassette coaching program on relationships from Ellen Kreidman called *Light His Fire, Light Her Fire*.

I was unaware that all of this was setting me on a trajectory to marry the man of my dreams and start my own personal development business.

"To love what you do and feel like it matters,
how could anything be more fun?"

— Katherine Graham

While still working in fashion, I married Tommy and eventually started a small business with two friends who were also colleagues. It really ignited my entrepreneurial spirit! I learned a lot. After a couple of years, I sold my share of the business to one of the partners. I had given birth to Christina by then and wanted to be home with her in her infant years. We were happy and life was good.

Then when Christina was just eighteen months old, Tommy had a serious health scare—stage three melanoma. At first, the news kept getting more dire. The cancer moved to his lymph nodes. I had always planned to get back to work, but I wanted to wait until Christina was two or three since Tommy traveled often. With his health taking a sharp turn, I enrolled Christina in preschool and started selling advertising for a luxury home magazine. This gave me flexibility.

I met two designers during this venture who ended up hiring me the following year to do public relations and marketing for them. I even started traveling a bit myself, since some of our clients were athletes who moved around a lot. I found a wonderful nanny, Graciela, who was truly an angel and became a special part of our family.

Tommy wanted to keep his diagnosis private, so we did. Graciela was the only one who knew, and she became my rock. We eventually got through his health scare with much faith and trust, thank God!

"Faith is not belief without proof, but trust without reservation."

— D. Elton Trueblood

As we watched our little girl grow and start elementary school, life was moving in a positive direction.

Shortly after Christina started school, my older sister Marie found out her cancer had moved to her bones. She was given about ten years to live. After coming to terms with that possibility, Marie regrouped and decided to do everything she could to live as healthily as possible.

But a few months later, Marie started having unbearable headaches. And then, just as summer was ending and school was starting up again, she was told her cancer had moved to her spinal fluid. It was a shock. If she did chemo, she may have eight months to a year, and if she did not, she'd likely have eight weeks to live. Everything stopped in that moment. Life as we knew it changed. We faced the unknown with no compass to guide us.

I stopped working immediately, moved Marie and her two kids in (part time), and became a full-time caregiver overnight. Tommy was truly my rock. You really learn a lot about people in times like this. Tommy stepped up beyond what I could have imagined. He never—and I mean never—complained. He did whatever he needed to do and then some, which is a whole story in itself. And again, deep faith and trust got us through a very difficult and tumultuous time.

I met Tommy through Marie, and today I feel that while she may have brought us together unconsciously, somehow she intuitively knew we'd eventually be taking care of her and helping with her children.

"Intuition is seeing with the soul."

— Dean Koontz

My sister died eight months later. She was fifty. Her death stopped me in my tracks and changed my focus. After caring for her and learning to navigate the intense and overwhelming feelings that come with doing so, I knew I wanted to be involved in patient advocacy.

This role was a huge shift into unknown territory for me. But it was pulling me, so I put myself into the healthcare field. I tried some new things that definitely stretched me and then landed in a start-up technology business for seniors and the disabled. The CEO created a position for me called

"Vice President of Relational Partnerships." I brought in thirteen partners and loved this new community.

Within eighteen months, they offered me a promotion to president. It didn't feel like a good fit for me and I liked my current position, so I said no. But after much nudging from the CEO, I finally agreed to it temporarily until we found a permanent fit. The CEO promised to work closely with me, so I thought I was up for the challenge and took the leap. At first it was great. Growing into this new position was truly invigorating.

Unfortunately, within a year, I found myself in a downward spiral. Our CEO went off the rails and I had to get the board together to quickly remove him from his position. Simultaneously, I found internal business issues that forced us to shut down the company altogether. The company's demise really messed with my confidence and self-esteem. I felt like a complete failure and a poor judge of character.

Though I wasn't an original founder, in becoming president, I felt completely responsible. I brought in help to properly shut things down and pay off our creditors, which we successfully did. I briefly thought I could start something new along similar lines, but it required too much time and funding. I promised myself I would never go after an entrepreneurial venture again. I felt I wasn't built for it.

"Life's challenges are not supposed to paralyze you; they're supposed to help you discover who you are."

— Bernice Johnson Reagon

When I turned fifty, I was thinking about my big sister Marie. Fifty years was all she got. Since I had been fortunate enough to have my health and all these experiences, why couldn't I do more? And then there was my daughter Christina, who was a teenager. What kind of role model would I be for her? I felt a fire igniting in me and decided it was time to jump in and really go for it this time.

But what would I do? I wanted to do something meaningful to me, something where I could make a difference. I initially thought of healthcare, but I was now disconnected from that path. I tried to be open to things, though I was feeling pretty vulnerable. Then my dear friend Sherri, a women's empowerment coach, asked if I would be interested in doing some marketing while I was figuring out my what's next. I said yes, and just like that, I was hooked. I forgot how much I loved personal development, though I had never thought of making a career of it.

Sherri told me I'd make a great coach, but at that time, I wasn't really interested in being a coach. Honestly, still feeling vulnerable and bruised from my last experience, I didn't believe I could coach anyone at the time. My confidence had taken a big hit. But I loved working in personal development and kept an open mind.

Later, I realized I needed my own immersion in personal growth to help me heal and move forward.

"Efforts and courage are not enough without purpose and direction."

— John F. Kennedy

For the past couple of years, Sherri had invited me to attend a weekend personal development event called DreamBuilder Live, but the timing had never seemed right. Being an amazing friend and beautiful soul, through her loving persistence, I finally agreed to go as her guest that January 2016.

The event could not have better fit the headspace I was in. It was life-changing and ignited something deep inside me. I am ever so grateful for my friendship with Sherri—she truly is my soul sister. After the event, I decided to invest in an online program, which was my first step in rebuilding my confidence.

In the meantime, I met Felicia, a life coach and results expert, and attended one of her local workshops. I instantly connected with her and her story. Realizing I could use a good mentor, I took her on as my coach.

I made up my mind to invest in myself more deeply and really figure out my what's next. As my walls came down, I realized I was absolutely drawn to coaching and intuitively knew it was my what's next evolution.

I had to let go of my old identity, of the failure I had just experienced, and embrace this new identity that ignited my spirit. I realized I was absolutely built to be a coach and an entrepreneur.

After working six months with Felicia, I made the brave and bold decision to enroll in The Life Mastery Institute to get certified as a life coach. It was a significant financial investment, but well worth it. Working with Felicia and then with Mary Morrissey and her amazing team was an integral part of arriving at this next level in my what's next evolution, for which I am deeply grateful.

And like clockwork, as soon as I decided to step into the next best version of myself, my old paradigms showed up to try to pull me back into my comfort zone. Family is very important to me, and deep down, I felt my career would somehow keep me from being there for my family. It was a fear I didn't realize I had at the time. My paradigm showed up as soon as I decided and made the financial investment in getting my coaching certification.

"You are going to often find that to step into your biggest opportunity, you will be asked to move through your biggest fear or insecurity."

— Ali Brown

On June 1, 2016, my mom's health suddenly took a bad turn. I jumped on a plane to Michigan and was back in the caregiving role with my younger sister Carrie, who flew in from Florida. That same month, June 17, Mom died, exactly one week before her eighty-third birthday. It was a very emotional time, but I was so grateful to have had the opportunity to be there with her and my family. She had a very peaceful passing.

When I got back home to Los Angeles, most interestingly, I found because I had a clear path I was committed to, I was able to jump right back into my studies and still be on track for my September certification.

Carrie and I both planned to meet back in Michigan in mid-July to check in on Dad and help him go through Mom's things before my September coaching training session started. We bought our tickets and were scheduled to leave on July 14. Early Sunday morning on July 10, I was awakened by a phone call. Just three weeks after Mom's passing, my oldest brother Jim called to tell me his twenty-year-old daughter (his only child), my niece and goddaughter, was killed on Saturday night in a tragic accident in Baltimore while crossing the street with friends. It was truly unimaginable, devastating, and incredibly heartbreaking.

Our entire family was still processing Mom's death, and now this tragic blow. It was mid-July, and I was back on a plane to Michigan for another family funeral. Our relatives and friends were shocked. We had all just gathered and said goodbye to Mom, but this was a different level of sadness and loss.

"We must embrace pain and burn it as fuel for our journey."

— Kenji Miyazawa

When I got back home later that month, I was left unsure what all this meant or why it all had happened. Surprisingly, though, I found I had an even deeper desire to pursue my path, rather than using the perfect excuse to let it go. My why had never been more clear or meaningful.

Family is very important to me, and so is continuing to evolve in a way that inspires my daughter, my family, my community, and the next generation to ignite their what's next best version while making a lasting impression on the world. Every moment is precious, and none of us know how long we have. Mom got eighty-two years, my sister got fifty, and my niece got twenty. Whatever gives you life and feeds your soul is calling you to wake up, stretch yourself, and get moving!

If not now, then when? Lean in to what's important to you. There is no time like the present to jump into a fuller life and step into your what's next evolution—your next best version. You're growing or you're dying every day. It's your choice. I made the choice to forge ahead, and I finished preparing for my certification. Even in the wake of such sadness and loss, my why had fuel and kept me going. That September, I officially became a life coach and opened up my business, Patti Smith Innovative Coaching, LLC.

"Character cannot be developed in ease and quiet. Only through experience of trial and suffering can the soul be strengthened, ambition inspired, and success achieved."

— Helen Keller

As difficult as all of this loss was, it taught me the power of having a clear vision and the importance of knowing and grounding it in why it's important to you. Your vision is your compass and your why is your fuel. When you have strong conviction, it will keep you moving forward even when your circumstances and current paradigms try to pull you back. We don't always have control over what happens, but we absolutely have control over what we make of it. And with a strong why, you'll have a solid foundation. Know what's most important to you, embrace it, and live each day by it.

So now you have established a strong foundation in Part I of this book by connecting with that authentic place in you that gives you life and sparks your soul's purpose. You have also gained an understanding of the value of shifting your mindset to one of possibility, and you have learned that the power to move forward requires you to let go of old limiting paradigms. You now have the motivation to step into the leading role of your life script, which connects directly to your core values, and you have a true understanding of your *why* and the deep meaning it carries for you.

You are now ready for the Seven Step IgniteU System in Part II, which will give you simple strategies to follow in creating your vision for your *what's next evolution*!

> *"If you can tune into your purpose and really align with it, setting goals so that your vision is an expression of that purpose, then life flows much more easily."*

> — Jack Canfield

Inspired Insight:

_____

_____

_____

_____

What is your *why* story?

_____

_____

_____

_____

"Anything and everything you have experienced has been purposeful; it has brought you to where you are now."

— *Iyanla Vanzant*

Inspired Action:

Take a minute to pose the question to yourself: What do I believe at my core? What's most important to me, and what do I deeply value? Here's a list of some core values. Circle those that resonate strongest with you, and then narrow the list down to the five words you are most aligned with.

Love	Variety	Loyalty	Fairness
Wealth	Calmness	Reason	Creativity
Family	Freedom	Independence	Relaxation
Morals	Fun	Achievement	Safety
Success	Recognition	Beauty	Acceptance
Knowledge	Nature	Spirituality	Friendships
Power	Popularity	Respect	Trustworthiness
Charity	Responsibility	Peace	Diversity
Free Time	Honesty	Stability	Leadership
Adventure	Humor	Wisdom	Professionalism

Balance	Challenge	Flexibility	Ethics
Security	Innovation	Learning	Advocacy
Joy	Appreciation	Service	Compassion
Collaboration	Well-Being	Understanding	Teamwork
Vision	Simplicity	Proactivity	Risk Taking
Traditionalism	Uniqueness	Resilience	Optimism
Accountability	Performance	Kindness	Decisiveness
Curiosity	Happiness	Contribution	Originality
Growth	Collaboration	Humor	Recognition
Dedication	Mindfulness	Community	Quality
Preparedness	Excellence	Empathy	Generosity
Caring	Responsiveness	Advancement	Passion
Grace	Humility	Versatility	Resourcefulness
Boldness	Commitment	Autonomy	Enthusiasm

"Effectiveness without values is a tool without a purpose."

— Edward de Bono

PART II

THE 7 STEP SYSTEM FOR LEADING A LIFE THAT LIGHTS YOU UP

The IgniteU System

1 - Inspire Your Imagination

2 - Get Clear on What You Want and Why

3 - Nail Down Your Decision to Go for It

4 - Invite in Support from Like-Mind People and Mentors

5 - Take Inspired Action Every Day

6 - Embrace Gratitude Throughout Your Journey

7 - Unite with a New Self-Image

?

CHAPTER 6

1-INSPIRE YOUR IMAGINATION

"Imagination is more important than knowledge. For knowledge is limited to all we know and understand, while imagination embraces the entire world, and all there ever will be to know and understand."

— Albert Einstein

R emember playing make believe when you were a child? Think about how often back then you used the powerful mental faculty that is your imagination. It tapped into your creativity, provoking you to step into a magical version of someone you wanted to be and to experience. Your imagination allowed you to dream and discover all sides of yourself with a freedom and abandon that opened up ideas and possibilities. Just like a white canvas ready to be painted, a blank new chapter ready to be inked, or a fresh set of blueprints ready to be designed, imagination begins the process. You start out tapping into it naturally as a kid, without hesitation. That is until the outside world begins telling you it's time to be realistic. You're told to stop dreaming and get real. With that kind of thinking, this abundant, expansive universe that offered endless possibility shrinks down to a sparse, constrictive planet earth with countless boundaries and limitations.

"Developing our imagination, the language of the soul, allows
Spirit to work through us as we answer our calling."

— Linda Naiman

The good news about boundaries and limitations when it comes to your dreams is they don't exist unless you actually believe they do. What you believe is possible becomes your reality. Society influences the world with this backward perspective, which causes you to live from the outside-in, looking to your outside conditions and circumstances to determine your fate. Yet you were actually designed to live from an inside-out perspective, looking within and connecting with your soul to discover what gives you your inspiration, a life you create by your own individual, authentic design. You are an evolving being, always creating a life. It's either by your specific design or by default based on outside conditions and circumstances. Trust what's trying to come through you.

"Whatever we plant in our subconscious mind and nourish with repetition and emotion will one day become a reality."

— Earl Nightingale

How we use our imagination lays the foundation for our future and begins to determine our path. And since everything starts in our mind, and we think in pictures, we can see how important our imagination is.

Think about everything around you. All of the inventions you know were once just ideas in someone's imagination. The clothes you're wearing, the home you live in, the car you drive, the bed you sleep in, your computer, your cell phone, the internet—all started out in someone's thoughts. It had to be imagined first before pen could even be put to paper, starting out as an idea and coming from a question. What would happen if…or how can I improve on…or how could I do that differently…or what if I could…?

It makes sense that if everything starts in our mind and our ideas come through our imagination, then this powerful tool is a necessity for forward movement and our what's next evolution. But we have a choice in how we direct it. As we become adults, it seems we often start using this powerful mental faculty to terrorize ourselves more than to inspire ourselves. We move into worst-case scenarios in our mind when we allow fear, doubt, anxiety, and worry to creep in.

"Worry is a misuse of imagination."

— Dan Zadra

When we were young, we inspired our imagination by asking lots of questions that started with "What if?" As we grew into the world, we started unconsciously allowing our circumstances and conditions to define us. The questions more often became, "Why do bad things always happen to me? Why can't I find my soulmate? How am I ever going to make enough money? How am I ever going to be happy?" And we shut down the possibility of "What if?" because we were so focused on asking ourselves "Why me?" and "How am I ever to…?" And when we find we don't have an answer, we say, "I guess it's just not meant to be."

That very constrictive energy can quickly take you down the rabbit hole of despair and victimhood. There's no movement forward coming from that place. But when you come from possibility and what if, it's expansive energy. That's the power of tapping into your imagination in a way that serves you through a powerful yet simple question: What would I love? That question is meant to guide you by inspiring you to follow a path that lights you up, gives you life, and has deep meaning. Think and focus on the result you would love and put the *how* on hold in your mind.

"Limitations live only in our minds. But if we use our imaginations, our possibilities become limitless."

— Jamie Paolinetti

I worked with a client who volunteered on Saturdays as a docent at the J. Paul Getty Museum in Los Angeles. She loved doing it. I had not yet been to the new Getty to see its vast art and beautiful collections, so she generously offered to give me a private tour. I was so thrilled to have her as my guide. Watching someone light up doing something they loved in an environment they loved was truly magical.

She told me the story of how the Getty came to be. Richard Meier was the lead architect back in the early '80s. He was selected from thirty-three architects invited to submit designs. The pool was narrowed down to seven and then three candidates. Meier's ability to share his vision of working with the natural landscape captured the selection committee's imagination.

Meier started with a hilltop (his blank canvas) in the Santa Monica Mountains right off the 405 freeway. He would sit on the mountain opposite the parcel and just stare at the empty space, allowing his imagination to flow. Tapping into his imagination and the expansive energy of "What if?", he wondered, *What do I see?* And then by putting pen to paper, the magnificent Getty was born with such beautiful detail and intention behind absolutely everything. The project faced many challenges, but when you come from possibility, anything is truly possible and can be figured out. Meier allowed his imaginative spirit to open up and flow through him. And the result was absolutely magnificent.

"Imagination creates reality."

— Richard Wagner

When you start creating anything, you are making it up until you give it form—reality—so when people tell you to stop dreaming, don't oblige. Dreams begin in the imagination. And you ignite your imagination with a high frequency question that comes from the energy of possibility such as, "What would I love to create?", and then focusing on as much detail and specificity as possible. Napoleon Hill, author of *Think and Grow Rich*, describes the imagination as the workshop of the mind. I love that. It's where ideas are shaped and take form.

This powerful mental faculty functions in two forms. One is called synthetic imagination, and the other is creative imagination. The synthetic imagination is when one takes old ideas and improves them. For example, the chair was invented simply as a place to sit. Think of all the variations that came from creating a place to sit—swivel chairs to move around your desk/office more easily, recliners to relax and stretch out in, high-chairs for babies to be supported in, the love seat to cozy up with a loved one in…and the list goes on. The chair was an original idea that continues to be improved on and expanded. That's using the synthetic imagination.

With creative imagination one taps into the Infinite Source, Universal

Intelligence. That is where insights, hunches, and inspiration come from and where new ideas are developed and formed. It is where the vision for your life is born. No one can see what you see. It's what comes naturally and inspires you in the form of deep desire. This demonstrates the importance of a strong *why* and how it aligns with the image you would love to bring into form as was discussed in the previous chapter. When you allow yourself the freedom to use your imagination to serve your burning desire to create and evolve what lights you up inside, the power of possibility is boundless. You've been given such a powerful gift, and used properly, it will absolutely continue to serve your growth and fulfillment. And the best part is that there's no age limit on the imagination.

> *"We don't stop playing because we grow old.*
> *We grow old because we stop playing."*
>
> — George Bernard Shaw

Remember, your vision is your dream. It's what inspires you and motivates you. You can either allow your dream to expand your ideas or allow your circumstances to contract them and put boundaries around them. When you allow your imagination to be open to anything and everything that lights you up inside, it becomes your intention and your compass.

To lean into your vision and open your imagination, learn to ask a high-frequency question. Rather than asking what you think is possible, ask,

"What would I love to create and feel in my life and who would I love to be?"

And let your imagination run free....

"Children see magic because they look for it."

— Christopher Moore

Inspired Insight:

_____

_____

_____

_____

Inspired Action:

Write down inspired ideas that come to you when you think about a life you are in love with:

(Think of these areas: health and wellbeing, relationships, vocation/creative expression/work in the world, income, time freedom, giving back.)

_____

_____

_____

_____

"If you fall in love with the imagination, you understand that it is a free spirit. It will go anywhere, and it can do anything."

— Alice Walker

CHAPTER 7

2-GET CLEAR ON WHAT YOU WANT AND WHY

"Clarity is the key to unlock your potential."

— Ruth Saw

The core of my mission is helping people ignite what truly gives them life and uncovering what's next for them so they continue to evolve on their personal journey. What's next is typically where most people get stuck. They don't know what they want, and they aren't sure why they're here.

How often have you seen the message, "Follow your passion and purpose"? Sounds great, but what does it really mean? Passion is what inspires you and lights you up—your desire, your vision—tapping into the ideas, talents, and assets inside you, pulling you to realize your dreams and share them in the world. It's your aiming point, what you want. Bob

Proctor always said, "Goals aren't for getting, they're for growing." That's why you want to work with a big idea, your vision of what you would love. Something that will stretch you into your next best version.

Purpose is the heart and soul of your dream. It's formed from your core values, what's most important to you—your why. This concept was introduced in Chapter 5 where we looked at connecting with your why through your life story. Clarity of purpose creates a solid foundation to build on. Purpose is what helps you navigate life by anchoring you in the deep meaning it represents for you, helping to ground and guide your choices.

"Finding clarity is eliminating options and aligning with values."

— Leadership Freak

Clarity is power! When you're clear about the result you want, you have a goal to move toward; you have a direction. When you have a strong conviction behind your goal, you have a purpose. It's critical to be crystal clear about what you truly want to manifest and then ground it in a strong belief in why it's important to you. It is what's required to bring about your vision and dreams.

What exactly are you looking for in your health and wellbeing? Describe the kind of relationships you'd like to have and with whom. What kind of income would you love to earn? (Be specific.) What type of work would you enjoy? Where would you love to explore and vacation? How would you love to give back? And then ask yourself: Why is it important, and why does it really matter? This is crucial to know because as you start acting on your goals and dreams, you will be tested.

When you step outside of your comfort zone, your current paradigms are waiting, ready to hold you back. These are the habits that want to keep you safe. Your limiting paradigms will show up as distractions, accidents, sickness, fear, doubt, worry, and even disguised as naysayers. Your limiting paradigms have a strong pull and are trying to keep you in your comfort zone, where it's safe and predictable.

Each of us has our own set point just like a thermostat. Our comfort level might be seventy-five degrees, so when conditions begin to get warmer or cooler, the heat or air conditioner kicks in to bring the temperature back to the comfortable setting.

Limiting paradigms work in a similar way. When you decide to step out of your comfort zone and do something new, your limiting paradigms show up to try to bring you back to where you're comfortable. It's your why that will continue to breathe life and meaning into your dream. That clarity of vision and defined purpose will keep you focused and help you get back on track when your paradigms start tossing you off course (and they will).

"Efforts and courage are not enough without purpose and direction."

— John F. Kennedy

You will live the next twelve months creating a life. Will it be driven by your vision and dream or driven by your conditions? A clear vision serves as a lighthouse to guide you on your course, while your why becomes the anchor to keep you grounded when the waters get rough. It's like a business plan is to a business. Your vision is the plan to your life. And your why is the centerpiece that keeps it together by grounding it with meaning.

Remember to start by asking yourself, "What would I love?" Not "What would I like?" or "What's practical?" or "What would others want?" The question is "What would I love?" That question has an igniting energy and only you can answer it. And with clarity and conviction, you will start to notice how aligning your passion and your purpose provides a common thread for your life to help lead you to your truth and your what's next evolution.

"Only when we are in alignment with our soul purpose
do we find true joy and inner peace."

— Anthon St. Maarten

When I was twenty-two, I decided to move to California from Michigan to expand my opportunities in the fashion industry. It was exciting yet scary to leave my family and friends and everything I'd known—leaving my comfort zone. My destination was clear—Los Angeles, California, which offered more possibilities and connections in the apparel business. I was clear about my why, which was to further my growth and find more opportunities in the fashion industry.

I had a place to live for free for the first month and a job interview when I got there. Was I scared? Yes, but my burning desire (my why) to do more in the fashion business, which I loved, was greater than my fear. The evening before I was to leave—I was driving to California—my car was parked in front of our house when a vehicle crashed into it. I was no longer leaving the next morning. Instead, I was heading to the body shop (distraction—limiting paradigm).

"Lack of clarity creates chaos and frustration. Those emotions are poison to any living goal."

— Steve Maraboli

My friends told me my car getting hit might be a sign I should stay in Michigan (limiting paradigm—naysayers). I considered it for a moment (limiting paradigm—self-doubt), but again, my burning desire was strong, so I shrugged it off.

Two weeks later, my car was fixed. The next morning, I drove off, ready to forge my new path. I turned onto the main road, and just a few miles down, my car overheated (limiting paradigm—distraction showing up as car trouble). I wasn't far from the dealership, so I drove straight there.

The limiting paradigms started coming on strong—were my friends right? Was this a sign? I was pretty conflicted, but again, my burning desire (my why) was stronger than my trepidation, and with a clear destination in front of me (California), I waited for my car to be fixed and took off. With $300 in cash to my name, a job interview at a Los Angeles apparel company, and a place to live for the first month for free, I finally took off for the West Coast.

A friend drove to California with me to keep me company. We made it to Los Angeles in a few days. On the way, we slept in the car one night and stayed in a flea bag hotel another night. Again, with a burning desire and a clear destination, I persevered and was able to create a very successful career in the fashion industry, which I loved. I have now been in California for over thirty years. I knew so little about the place where I was going or exactly how I'd live, but I wanted it so badly and committed to doing whatever it took to lean into my next best version of what ignited my heart and soul. I never looked back. Yes, the limiting paradigms showed up and taunted me, but I learned something key. Clarity gives you the power to shine light on your passion, bringing it into focus as your purpose fuels it with deep meaning aligned with your values. This gives you the ability to stare down any limiting paradigm in your path. I was clear about what I wanted and why it was important to me.

I'd like to close this chapter with a quote by Abraham-Hicks:

Clarity is alignment.
Clarity is a clear impulse of where to go.
Clarity is trusting the path.
Clarity is not standing in a wobbly place.
Clarity is the momentum that has no resistance, and when you're in that place of clarity, the feeling of what to do next is right there.

Inspired Insight:

_____

_____

_____

_____

Inspired Action:

Review the inspired ideas you wrote down using your imagination in the previous chapter. What jumps off the page at you? Zero in on it and specifically describe what your related *want* looks like in each area of your life and describe *why* it's important to you.

_____

_____

_____

_____

> *"Clarity is like casting light. Clarity allows us to see better and eases the path of understanding."*
>
> — Cyrus Panjvani

> *"When you find your why, you don't hit snooze! You find a way to make it happen!"*
>
> — Eric Thomas

?

CHAPTER 8

3-NAIL DOWN YOUR DECISION TO GO FOR IT

"The only person you are destined to

become is the person you decide to be."

— Ralph Waldo Emerson

With a clear vision (your dream) and a strong purpose (your why), the next step is to make up your mind to go for the life you've designed and have a burning desire to manifest. This is commitment time. It's about closing the door on the idea of *maybe I'll make it happen* and claiming that *Absolutely, I can and I will make this happen—period.* Deciding is what strikes the match to move you forward. And it's often at this very juncture, when most people allow fear to get in the way, that they halt the dream. That's when you allow the outside to come inside and cloud your vision and focus. It's when doubt creeps in and causes you to start the second-guessing process. And right around the corner come the excuses: *I can't do this. Who do I think I am to...?* or *Why not wait until I'm ready?* "Getting ready" is a *stalling tactic.* You're fooling yourself with this idea. If you are waiting until you *feel* ready, you will never *be* ready. The only way you will move toward a result you want is by making a move. And that starts with deciding to go for what you would love.

I once was at a real crossroad in making a career decision. I was at the pinnacle of happiness working for a top fashion company with great colleagues, a supportive management team, and an awesome work environment. When my colleagues and I traveled to New York, we always stayed at the trendiest hotels. We dined at top restaurants and worked in beautiful showrooms in Los Angeles, San Francisco, and Manhattan. The company spared no expense to provide a creative and beautiful environment and was always innovating. Almost every day I went to work, I felt inspired and motivated. One day, I received a phone call from an up-and-coming company. They had received my name from someone as a referral and wanted to know if I was interested in interviewing with them. I was happy to set up a meeting, but not really looking to make a move. After quite an interview process, I was offered the job. Part of me was honored at the invitation, but another part was not. I felt very conflicted. *Why now?* I thought. *Just when everything is going so well. I'm in such a sweet spot with my work, so content and comfortable.* That was the first time in my career when I was at a fork in the road.

"Learn to trust the journey, even when you do not understand it. Sometimes what you never wanted or expected turns out to be what you need."

— marcandangel.com

I really didn't know what I would do. But I knew I had to make a decision. I considered my current work environment, which fit me well, but here was this new opportunity. I felt really stuck. At the suggestion of my boyfriend (now hubby), I made a pros and cons list for each company. I was shocked at what my list revealed. All the main reasons I wanted to stay at the current company were personal, yet the majority of the reasons to make a change were in service to evolving my career. I instantly knew making the move was the way to go. It was a really tough decision, but I went for it! The pace was different, the management team was tough, and there was a mix of interesting characters. The first couple of weeks, I wasn't sure I had made the right move, but I quickly got into sync and realized it was exactly what I needed to grow. I hit my stride at a whole new level.

Interestingly enough, six months after my move, the company I left was sold. New management came in and let go of some of the very people I worked for, as well as some of my favorite colleagues. Those who remained told me the environment had changed drastically. All the reasons I would have stayed were now gone. The Universe sure works for you if you trust it and pay attention to the path it's revealing…and decide on your next best step. Don't let indecisiveness keep you from personal growth and development. Be aware that indecision opens you up to allowing outside conditions to get inside of you and control your outcome. So, if you're not clear about and committed to the result you want, when your limiting beliefs show up (and they will) in the form of excuses, they will fight hard to justify themselves and keep you in the comfort zone of status quo. That's not living; that's existing…which is not progress or evolution.

The truth is we all have the capacity to be effective decision makers. We develop this skill through experience, and with experience, comes wisdom. The reality is nobody but you knows what's best for you. You are responsible for your own life and making decisions for yourself, in service to what gives you life and purpose. The word decision comes from the Latin word, *decidere*, which is a combination of two words, *de* meaning off and *caedere* meaning cut, which means to cut something off. When you decide, you cut off everything except the things that truly matter. It's like when you have a beautiful piece of fabric you'd love to make a garment from. You first have to design a pattern (like your dream) of what you want—a blouse, trousers, a dress. Then you place the pattern on the fabric and cut out the pieces that will form the final product of what you want. You cut off and discard the remnants you don't need. Cut off and release the thoughts (old patterns) that don't serve your dream.

Since our life is truly about our evolution, which is a process, part of that process is continuing to make decisions to move us forward—whether in our professional or personal lives.

"Decisions are the frequent fabric of our daily design."

— Don Yaeger

My sister Marie was an inspiration to me as I watched her decide to go for what gave her life while she was fighting for her life. Marie was a mechanical engineer in the first chapter of her career. Later, when her kids were in school, she decided to go back to college to earn a second degree as a landscape architect, which combined her creativity and her love of nature.

Soon after she started school, cancer crept back into her life and her marriage began falling apart. Rather than giving up school, she dove in. Even when family and friends (naysayers with good intentions) encouraged her to put school on hold while she underwent radiation and chemotherapy, she decided to continue her studies. Sometimes she just couldn't make it to school, but she always made up the work. She amazed me by earning that degree against the odds.

Marie chose what filled her up, which kept her focused on something positive. She decided to pursue her dream with a deep commitment and a strong will, knowing nothing was going to stop her. And what a great example she was for her children in showing commitment no matter the circumstances. Her courage—to step into the unknown, to focus, and to decide to endure through disease and a divorce—fueled her will to finish, and she did.

"Courage isn't having the strength to go on, it is going on when you don't have the strength."

— Napoleon Bonaparte

Marie worked for some smaller design firms for a while, but they were unable to offer good medical insurance. Not knowing what was ahead, she decided to find work at a larger firm. She got a job at Valley Crest in its commercial division. Within a couple of years of her terminal cancer diagnosis, she had great health insurance, which provided high-quality options and care. Valley Crest kept her on its payroll for quite a while and really worked with her. The company and her coworkers showed her empathy. The owners had lost a daughter to breast cancer years earlier and had started a foundation called We Spark. The team she worked with was like a little family where she felt love and support. All of this was a result of decisions Marie made that served her in ways she never imagined. The Universe works with you and for you when you allow it to. And that starts with having the courage to decide to listen to your inner self.

"Opportunities are like sunrises. If you wait too long, you miss them."

— William Arthur Ward

In the spring of 2000, my husband Tommy, who traveled abroad a lot, asked me if I'd like to go to Italy with him. This time it would be for fun. We would take the train from Milan to Florence to Venice to Rome. I'd never been to Italy, so it sounded exciting and romantic. We talked about going in the fall when the weather would be beautiful, but we needed to coordinate our work schedules to see if we could both take the time off.

We needed to decide quickly to get everything booked. We picked October. I was still on straight commission. October was a very busy time for me with some larger clients, so I was having a difficult time accepting being gone for two weeks. I was more focused on my struggle and concern than what I would love and the options if I could make this work. I was torn, unsure what to do.

Tommy finally said, "If this isn't a good time for you, then let's put it off and wait until next year." By remaining in conflict energy, I was allowing my condition (conflict) to make the decision for me. Fortunately, I sought support from a like-minded colleague and friend, Sherri, who was all about travel and adventure!

When I told Sherri I was probably going to put off our Italy trip until the following year, she asked me if I would love to go this year or next? I told her I'd love to go this year, of course. When I said it was "bad timing," she said, "Who knows what might come up next year?" She said if I truly wanted to make it work, I could. "Just decide you're going to take the trip to Italy and book it (inspired action)."

With the help of my amazing office manager Maureen, we figured out how to ensure my clients would be taken care of while I was gone. And to top it off, Sherri offered me a 50 percent off coupon for a Sheraton Hotel that she couldn't use before it expired. Wouldn't you know, Lido Island in Venice, which was an absolutely beautiful location, had a Sheraton Hotel. That trip was an incredible experience for Tommy and me. I did not have one regret. When I came back, my accounts were still there and doing fine.

The craziest thing was, the following fall, something we never could have imagined happened—the September 11 terrorist attacks. We would not have traveled that October. And the year after that, I was pregnant with our daughter Christina. A year after she was born, Tommy had a serious health scare. I'm so happy and grateful I didn't default to putting off my decision to go to Italy with my husband.

"The hard thing when you get old is to keep your horizons open.
The first part of your life everything is in front of you, all your
potential and promise. But over the years, you make decisions;
you can carve yourself into a given shape. Then the challenge is
to keep discovering the green growing edge."

— Howard Thurman, Civil Rights Leader

When you imagine something you would love and then clarify what it looks like specifically, the next step is to decide to do that very thing. Make up your mind and claim it with inspired action. Once you do, you will feel empowered by possibility. Understand that you will be at the green growing edge of your evolution with your limiting paradigms. This is when the second guessing, the self-doubt, the anxiety about the unknown, and the naysayers will show themselves.

This brings us to the next powerful step, which we'll look at in the following chapter—creating a support structure to support your vision and dreams.

"Live in the present. The past is gone; the future is unknown—but
the present is real, and your opportunities are now."

— Maxwell Maltz

Inspired Insight:

_____

_____

_____

_____

Inspired Action:

Make a "committed decision" to go after a life that lights you up. Write that decision here. For example, "I can and I will go for the dream that's igniting me and my what's next evolution, and nothing or no one is going to stop me because this is a part of who I am and my truth."

_____

_____

_____

_____

"You cannot make progress without making decisions."

— Jim Rohn

CHAPTER 9

4- INVITE IN SUPPORT FROM LIKE-MINDED PEOPLE AND MENTORS

*"Deliberately seek the company of people who influence
you to think and act on building the life you desire."*

— Napoleon Hill

I n the 1930s, Andrew Carnegie, one of the wealthiest men at the time, commissioned a young writer named Napoleon Hill to study the habits of successful people. Hill then wrote about his findings in *Think and Grow Rich*. One thing Hill discovered was his subjects tended to create groups he came to call "Mastermind Groups." The members of a mastermind group are focused on helping each other "be" in a higher mind—a mind coming from a solution mindset rather than a problem mindset. Hill explained that when two or more people get together to access answers and support, it's almost as if a third mind is created from the group.

"Surround yourself with people who have dreams, desire, and ambition; they'll help you push for and realize your own."

— Anonymous

Alone we get stuck in our circumstances and conditions, so it's difficult to think beyond our blocks on our own. But when two or more people come together, you have access to ideas and information you may not find on your own. The goal of a mastermind group is to come together with "partners in believing." They don't judge, criticize, or condemn. Rather they support you by helping you see where you've closed yourself off and by giving fresh perspective. The saying "It's hard to see the picture when you're in the frame" explains this idea.

Your partners in believing are not in your frame of mind. They're not in your conditions. What's crazy is you might not even realize you're actually holding on to a limitation. As you start to tell the group your story, they can stop you and say, "Why do you believe that? What if it didn't limit you?" It's helpful to have someone who supports you and isn't caught up in your conditions to give an honest perspective and provide specific, actionable suggestions.

"We all need someone who believes in us just a little bit more than we do ourselves in order for us to become stronger."

— Raphael Love

Often, confusion can stop us from moving forward by keeping us stuck in our problems. Our internal beliefs, which include our patterns and habits (our life as we relate to it), argue for the problem's existence. We want to learn to think beyond our problems and change our perception. This can be challenging on our own. The continued support of like-minded people and mentorship has allowed me to continue to evolve my what's next best version.

"You are a product of your environment. So, choose the environment that will best develop you toward your objective."

— W. Clement Stone

I must give a shout out to the *eWomen Network*, a group of ambitious, heart-centered, professional women entrepreneurs who truly motivated and encouraged me to spread my wings at a time when I was ready to settle for "whatever" rather than what inspired me. The ignite idea in this book was inspired in collaboration with two colleagues from this organization a few years ago. One was Toni, the managing director of our Calabasas chapter at the time and a diligent partner in believing.

When I started out on the speaking circuit, Toni showed up to support me. But more than that, she pushed me to my green growing edge as a speaker with constructive feedback. It helped me lose the comfort zone of my speaking notes and lean more into the message from my heart and soul, which flipped a switch in me as to how I connect with the audience. I trusted Toni and was open to her feedback. What a game changer for me. It's so important to find mentors and partners in believing who truly believe in you and want to support you in your what's next evolution.

"We all need people who will give us feedback. That's how we improve."

— Bill Gates

Every year now, I attend the eWomen Conference in Dallas where I can engage with many heart-centered women entrepreneurs who are like-minded and supportive of our businesses and each other. It's a place to collaborate and share ideas and resources to continue to grow and evolve our what's next best versions. One of the core values of this group is to "lift as we climb."

A young woman who lost her job shortly after joining our business community, through working with a mastermind group, launched her own business from an idea and her love of making cookies. When you have people helping you see past your circumstances and you reframe your limiting mindset by focusing on solutions rather than on the problem, the possibilities are endless.

I attended one of Mary Morrissey's DreamBuilder Live events a few years back with 800 people. We did an exercise where you partnered with someone. Then you each shared your dream as the other listened intently, holding the space for the speaker. My partner had to use the bathroom, so I just waited in the back. As I stood there taking in the energy of the room in that moment, it was intoxicating. How often are you in a large group of people where you get to be in such strong energy of pure possibility and support with absolutely no negativity, judgment, or sourness? Just pure expansive, positive, creative, and loving energy. It was absolutely invigorating. The power I felt in that room, I believe, could have moved mountains.

"Surround yourself with only people who are going to lift you higher."

— Oprah Winfrey

When Marie was in the last stage of her battle with cancer and being discharged from the City of Hope, the discharge nurse encouraged us to have my sister discharged into hospice care at our home. Of course, when we heard hospice, we thought of death. Even though we knew Marie was nearing the end of her life journey here on earth, hospice seemed so finite. But we remained open-minded and listened to the nurse, who had worked in hospice care.

The nurse explained how hospice care is so misunderstood. People can go into hospice, then do well and come out of it. It doesn't happen often, but it can happen. The nurse said the problem is most doctors don't suggest hospice until it's too late to receive the full benefits of it. She said to qualify for hospice, one needs a prognosis of six months or less to live, which Marie was given. She explained hospice is as much for the family as for the patient. The nurse said the only difference in care is when you bring hospice in, they are your medical team. Hospice has a main physician, but it's really the nurses and the additional support who are directly involved with the patient's care.

I was a bit nervous about letting go of the doctors we had come to know and count on, but I trusted this nurse and her compassionate conviction. And boy, was I glad I did.

Hospice became my team of like-minded support in a way I never could have imagined. Looking back, they truly were my healthcare mastermind. For any problem that came up with Marie, and I mean any problem, they were there to help us navigate solutions and options. And they always came to us in the home. Marie had access to massages, someone to help her bathe, a spiritual counselor, and if a problem arose, the nurses would come and not leave until Marie was resting comfortably.

I had no idea this was what hospice was about. They had counselors for Marie's kids and the rest of the family. They became almost like extended family. In fact, with all of the support, Marie's health stabilized enough so she was actually strong enough to attend her son's lacrosse game as well as her daughter's cross country meet.

When Marie was in her last days, the hospice nurse suggested I ask her if she wanted to talk to a priest, rabbi, or whomever. Marie had converted to Judaism years earlier, so I said she would want to talk to a rabbi. The nurse calmly persisted, saying I should ask Marie. I vehemently replied I already knew she'd want to speak with a rabbi and there was no way Marie would want to speak to a priest. That is what I thought. The nurse said I'd be surprised at what people want when they are near the end. She convinced me to be open and have the conversation.

Surprisingly, Marie wanted to speak to my priest, Father McNamara (Father Mac). She told me she had always wanted to meet him. She knew how much I enjoyed his sermons and how well he related to the people of the parish. She wanted him to come talk to her and give her the last rites. The nurse's suggestion to have that conversation was pivotal. And Marie's decision also helped our mother truly be at peace in such a difficult time. It opened my eyes, and I am truly grateful for that nurse's wisdom and persistence.

> *"We need people in our lives with whom we can be as open as possible. To have real conversations with people may seem like such a simple, obvious suggestion, but it involves courage and risk."*
>
> — Thomas Moore

Marie was out of it the day Father Mac was coming, and I warned him she wasn't very responsive. As soon as he walked into the room, however, she instantly sat up and started talking to him clearly. This went on for almost an hour. It was truly remarkable to witness her clarity in that conversation.

My mother, father, younger sister Carrie, and I sat around Marie as Father Mac gave her last rites. She was coherent and it was so beautiful.

Two days later, she passed away.

The hospice team was there through the end and stayed in touch with my parents and me for another year. They had great suggestions and resources to help us get through the grieving process. I never thought of our hospice team as a mastermind group, *per se*, but they were unwavering support, true partners in believing, and what I'm going to call my "Mastermind Angels."

> *"Anything is possible when you have the right*
> *people there to support you."*
>
> — Misty Copelan

The entire experience taught me you don't always know what you don't know because it's really hard to see the picture when you're in the frame of your circumstances. That's when being surrounded by like-minded people who understand and support you where you are, who are able and willing to help generate ideas and mastermind solutions even in a time of sadness and loss is such a gift when you're open to it. Little gifts can be found in the most difficult situations if you are open to allowing the support in.

"Make feedback normal. Not a performance review."

— Ed Batista

Many of us tend to "do it on our own." Sometimes that's fine. It's good to put yourself out there and challenge yourself. But having support when you feel stuck, hit a wall, get overwhelmed, or feel like you're in over your head and can't pull it together helps you move forward by offering a new perspective.

"Your dream comes from within you. Your
success comes from who's beside you."

— Sandra Yancey

Finding a mentor to guide you in achieving your goals and dreams can help accelerate your desired results and give you structured support and accountability. Think about an athletic coach. Elite athletes have them because they need the support that talent alone cannot sustain. They need someone who understands where they are, where they want to go, and can help them get there—if they're willing to be open, listen, and put in the effort.

> *"A good coach will make players see what they*
> *can be rather than what they are."*
>
> — Ara Parseghian

Create a support structure that can help you see past your blind spots and talk to you straight up, help you generate ideas, encourage you to continue with your goals and dreams, and hold you accountable.

> *"There is a frequency to successful living and achieving your dreams,*
> *and when you are able to surround yourself with exceptional people and*
> *creative people, you will automatically discover your genius zone."*
>
> — Christopher Cumby

Inspired Insight:

_____

_____

_____

_____

Inspired Action:

Find a partner in believing. Think about someone or a small group of heart-centered people who are encouraging and nonjudgmental. It could be someone you look up to like a mentor. A partner in believing is not someone who's going to tell you what to do, but someone who will help you see beyond your blind spots, encourage you, and hold you accountable on your journey.

"Surround yourself with good people, surround yourself with positivity and people who are going to challenge you to make you better."

— Ali Kreiger

CHAPTER 10

5-TAKE INSPIRED ACTION EVERY DAY

"Start where you are. Use what you have. Do what you can."

— Arthur Ashe

Nothing happens until you act because action changes things. My late father-in-law, who lived to be ninety-five, used to say, "You're growing or dying every day." And it is a choice. First, you have to be willing to trust your choices. It's important to listen to your intuition. Your personal growth only comes from trusting yourself. You can't allow the fear of making a big mistake, failing miserably, embarrassing yourself, or not doing something perfectly the first time to overshadow what you truly desire. Don't let your fears control you. Listen to your still, small voice and move forward. The only way to grow is to act. As the saying goes, practice makes perfect. Practice is action.

Through repeatedly acting, you gain experience. Yes, your actions will be imperfect for a while until you master taking action through practice.

An economics professor was permitted to do an experiment with a senior-level class. He told the students the first day they would be doing something different—pottery. He split the class into two groups. Group A would make one high quality pot which would be the basis for their entire grade. He gave them places to go to watch pottery being made, places to see great artists at work, etc. Group B was told their entire grade would be based on the quantity of pots they made. The professor repeated this experiment for three years. He found the best pots came from the quantity group every time. Put simply, it was really about just getting out there and getting your hands dirty. The more pots you make, the better you're going to get at it. Practice, practice, practice!

"When you are not practicing, remember, someone somewhere is practicing, and when you meet him, he will win."

— Ed Macauley

How does this story apply to your life? What have you been wanting to try but haven't yet? Don't overthink it. Trust your intuition and just get started; begin practicing by taking baby steps. What's most important is that whatever actions you begin to take are in alignment with your goals and dream. That's called an inspired action. Doing something new, something you've never done before, will most likely be an "imperfect" inspired action. That's okay. The hardest part is getting started.

Life is moving forward whether you are or not. Don't let excuses become your results. The week has seven days, and "someday" isn't one of them. No one knows what's around the corner. We have the day we are in, and we have the choice to act on that day or not. Don't let your life pass you by. Jump into what's next for you and start making some new moves.

> *"Inaction breeds doubt and fear. Action breeds confidence and courage. If you want to conquer fear, do not sit home and think about it. Go out and get busy."*
>
> — Dale Carnegie

When I was in my mid-twenties back in the late 1980s and working in the apparel business, an interesting opportunity dropped into my lap. I definitely wasn't looking for it, but I allowed my curiosity to take me forward. I didn't overthink it and kept an open mind. Tommy's best friend Earl was a race car driver looking for sponsorship. Tommy (who was my boyfriend at the time) suggested Earl ask me if the apparel company I worked for might consider sponsoring him. Curious and intrigued, I leaned into the possibility, which was the beginnings of much "imperfect" inspired action.

"Take the first step in faith. You don't have to see the whole staircase, just take the first step."

— Martin Luther King, Jr.

This journey was pivotal in opening me up to the idea of taking constant inspired action with no experience. I started by asking one of our marketing people some questions. From there, Earl and I came up with a strategy that would become a ten-million-dollar marketing campaign. Earl's friend Larry owned some Burger King franchises, and we came up with a ten-million dollar ad campaign to market through the kids' meals.

Larry suggested we align with a charity. I asked one of my roommates about charities that might be good to align with. She said one in particular always hit home with her—the Make-A-Wish Foundation. I had never heard of it, but after doing some research, I was inspired by its mission. Earl was instantly onboard and thrilled about aligning with this charity.

I reached out to Make-A-Wish and explained what we wanted to do, which was grant one of its kids' wishes to ride in a race car with a professional driver. We would fly the child's family in for the race as well. The experience would be videotaped with an in-car camera and given to the Make-A-Wish child to keep.

Make-A-Wish loved the idea!

The funding would come from 10 percent of each Burger King kids' meal sold, which would go to the Make-A-Wish Foundation.

"We make a living by what we get. We make a life by what we give."

— Winston Churchill

The next inspired action step was setting up a meeting with Mattel Toys to discuss purchasing a substantial number of toy race cars that would be put in each meal. Talk about imperfect action. This was all uncharted territory for me, but because I had a clear vision and mission, which were truly my compass and fuel, I pushed forward one baby step at a time.

Mattel was thrilled to participate. It had been trying to work with the Make-A-Wish Foundation for quite a while, and this was a perfect opportunity. How fortuitous.

Once I secured the price, I was ready for my next imperfect inspired action step—meeting with Burger King's top management team and its public relations firm Saatchi & Saatchi in New York City.

With the meeting set, a big problem surfaced. The meeting was scheduled for fashion market week when all the buyers were in Los Angeles. It was time for my next imperfect inspired action. I got creative and figured out how I could miss two days of market week and make the meeting with Burger King and Saatchi & Saatchi. Everything was settled, and we were back on track as planned—except....

The day before the meeting with Burger King, Mattel called. It had just signed an exclusive agreement with McDonald's, and unfortunately, could not participate in our campaign with Burger King. Mattel was truly disappointed, but it would be a big conflict of interest, so that was that. I thought, *This can't be happening!*

It was time for more imperfect inspired action. Earl and I asked ourselves, "What *can* we do with where we are using what we have?" An idea dropped in! What about Matchbox Cars instead of Mattel?

I quickly got on the phone with Matchbox, secured my price, and they were in. They FedEx overnighted Matchbox cars to my hotel room in New York City so I would have them for my presentation the very next day.

"Our chief want in life is somebody who will make us do what we can."

— Ralph Waldo Emerson

The meeting was a complete success, and we thought we were off to the races. In fact, while I was in New York, Earl got a call from Mitsubishi and he set up a meeting for me at the LA Auto Show when I got back to Los Angeles. They were not only going to supply tires for Earl's car, which is what he wanted, but they were also going to give away a car at the race— all in the name of our Make-A-Wish campaign.

We just had one more hurdle. The Burger King management I had met with said I needed to meet with their head marketing person, who was passing through Los Angeles, and he would make the final decision if they were going to move forward with our idea. Burger King was pivotal to the campaign since we were generating all of the funding to fulfill the Make-A-Wish grant through Burger King's kids meals. I met with him at the airport, another imperfect inspired action. I thought we were just tying up loose ends, but basically, he was not interested whatsoever. Unbeknownst to me, he shared that they were also considering a Bart Simpson campaign idea, which he seemed personally invested in already. Honestly, it seemed like he was just going through the motions with our meeting to appease the upper management whom I had met with and who loved our idea. But ultimately, the final decision was up to him since he was in charge of marketing, and he shut us down. This immediately ended the entire campaign. Make-A-Wish didn't entertain the race wish idea with the child until we had a firm deal, but it was still extremely disappointing that we could not make this happen for them.

The entire experience was an education and a growth opportunity. It taught me the value of passion, clarity of vision, and perseverance. And even without knowing a lot, by continuing to take "imperfect" inspired action steps in the direction of whatever was pulling me, taking action continued to open new opportunities. I couldn't believe what we did accomplish, and we met some pretty awesome people along the way. I also learned what you can do working with a community of like-minded people toward a greater goal.

After that, the entrepreneur bug took hold. The experience and learning to take imperfect inspired action has continued to embolden me and help me unravel my what's next evolution, fuel my why, and help me uncover the next best version of myself, supporting me in what I'm here to do and become.

> *"Coming together is a beginning, staying together is progress, and working together is success."*
>
> — Henry Ford

Making mistakes or failing at something leads to our biggest personal growth if we focus on doing instead of doing it perfectly and just doing the best we can in the moment. We do what we can, using what we have, right from where we are. Don't worry about being perfect; we learn from doing. Take the golden nuggets (what you've learned) from the experience and release the idea of the failure or mistakes.

When you allow failure or mistakes to teach you rather than break you, like a caterpillar transforms into a butterfly, you evolve into your next best version. It's the movement that creates the energy that will give you the result you desire. Practice, practice, practice, and you will continue to get better and become more confident in your endeavors. Focus on what you can do, and approach everything from that perspective every time.

When you're focused on the solution and take imperfect inspired action, you're not thinking about things going wrong. You're focused on forward movement—always forward! That's when the Law of Attraction comes in—like attracts like.

This applies to thought and action. Where your attention goes, energy flows. People and circumstances matching your thoughts and energy will come to you. You never know where opportunities are going to come from, but the main point is to understand you want to move toward making things happen. It's up to you to set the energy in motion.

"Success seems to be connected with action. Successful people keep moving. They make mistakes but don't quit."

— Conrad Hilton

For years, my older brother Jim worked in the legal field and absolutely loved it. At one point, however, he was put in a compromising position that challenged his integrity. Since he chose not to succumb, he quickly found himself out of work and needing to make a bold career move. His search was informed by a question that served possibilities and came from a solution mindset. How could he use his vast experience in a new field?

Jim made it his new job to find a new job. He got up every morning, laser-focused on going to work. He would get dressed, have breakfast, and then retreat into his home office at 9 a.m. to begin his workday, which consisted of looking for new opportunities, new possibilities.

Jim worked until 5 p.m., five days a week. He worked with headhunters. He went on countless interviews. He continued his job search himself, not waiting for the headhunters. Remarkably, he eventually landed a new job just a few miles from his home. It was a new position created for someone with his experience, but in a new area. Jim found it on his own through countless hours of searching through Indeed.com.

Jim found an executive, high-level position. I think the lesson here is you must continue to take imperfect inspired action and continue to put yourself and your energy out there, not knowing what will come back or where it will come from. But you get the energy aligning and moving in the direction of what you want to create.

"It's not what you do once in a while; it's what you do day in and day out that makes the difference."

— Jenny Craig

You know the saying, "Use it or lose it." A few years ago, I broke my wrist getting out of a hammock. I had never broken anything before, and it was incredibly painful. Unfortunately, it was my right wrist and I'm right-handed. Fortunately, I didn't need surgery, but I had a cast from my hand up to my shoulder. My right arm was completely immobilized. I had that cast for just three weeks before it was time to take it off and put on a smaller cast.

I thought when the cast came off, I'd feel some relief before getting into the next cast. But when the cast came off, the pain I felt was beyond intense! I thought something was wrong. The doctor took an x-ray and said my wrist was healing well, so I couldn't understand why I felt so much pain. The doctor explained atrophy was causing the pain. I couldn't believe it was so bad after just three weeks of immobility. He prescribed physical therapy after the final cast came off. I thought the therapy was for the break, but he explained it was for the atrophy.

What truly blew me away was this idea of use it or lose it. The physical body is made of energy and so is the world around us. We are meant to continue to evolve, grow, and move. Always forward. It hit me that it was like what Dad always said, "You've got to keep moving, even when you don't feel like it."

> "Dreams don't work unless you take action. The surest
> way to make your dreams come true is to live them."
>
> — Roy T. Bennett

Mom used to say if you need someone to help you get something done, ask someone who's busy, because they're in the habit of being active and will always find a way to make things happen. Don't wait. Take an imperfect inspired action step today. Understand the best way to move forward is to act, because without action, you can't get anywhere.

Remember:

Action

Changes

Things

> *"Knowledge is power: You hear it all the time, but
> knowledge is not power. It's only potential power. It only
> becomes power when we apply it and use it. Somebody
> who reads a book and doesn't apply it, they're at no
> advantage over someone who's illiterate. None of it works
> unless you work. We have to do our part. If knowing is
> half the battle, action is the second half of the battle."*
>
> — Jim Kwik

Inspired Insight:

_____

_____

_____

_____

Inspired Action:

Write down three to five imperfect actions you can and will take to move your dream forward.

_____

_____

_____

_____

"The big secret in life is that there is no big secret. Whatever your goal, you can get there if you're willing to work."

— Oprah Winfrey

CHAPTER 11

6-EMBRACE GRATITUDE THROUGHOUT YOUR JOURNEY

"A grateful attitude becomes a grid through which you perceive life."

— Sarah Young

S tarting each day grounded in the foundation of gratitude and appreciation is the best way to anchor your day. Everyone is a mass of energy operating on various frequencies. When you're being negative, you're operating on a constrictive low frequency. When you're being optimistic, you're operating on an expansive high frequency. Abundance is on a higher frequency, so if you would love to have more abundance, it's up to you to move yourself to a higher frequency.

Sometimes it's challenging to raise your energy when you're really feeling stuck in your circumstances. A great way to instantly move out of that low frequency is to put yourself in the frequency of gratitude. Do something nice for someone. Whether it's a heartfelt compliment, holding the door open, reaching out with a phone call, sending a thoughtful greeting card, paying for a stranger's coffee, or volunteering, showing gratitude is as easy as making a gesture of appreciation or performing a loving act of kindness. It's an instant energy shift because abundance and gratitude operate on the same high frequency.

My mentor Mary Morrissey told me about the idea of amplifying abundance in all areas to amplify gratitude and thankfulness for everything and everyone around you. Do that and you'll increase the abundance coming to you. It's not just about being grateful when things come easily or pleasantly. It's even more important to be grateful when it's not so easy. It's about looking for the good in situations and people even when why you'd be grateful isn't clear.

"Humans see what they want to see."

— Rick Riordan

When you get into the habit of looking for the good, you're focusing on staying on the frequency of gratitude, which is in alignment with abundance. Where your attention goes, energy flows. Focusing on what you are grateful for helps you look for the good and beauty in life and in the people around you. Remind yourself of your blessings. Get into the habit of looking for the good in all things, no matter how challenging or unpleasant they may seem. The practice of gratitude is powerful. It will instantly help ground you, and it is a beautiful place to live from every day.

"Be thankful for what you have; you'll end up having more. If you concentrate on what you don't have, you will never ever have enough."

— Oprah Winfrey

I love this story, true or not. The message is a beautiful one.

As the Christmas holidays approached, a teacher in a remote school, about sixty miles inland, told the children about giving "thoughtful gifts" to the people you care about and giving from the heart. The class wanted to try this and decided to exchange gifts. On the last day of school before Christmas, one of the students gave the teacher a gift wrapped in a leaf. It was a seashell. The teacher was delighted but curious as to how the student got the seashell.

"I walked to the ocean and picked up the shell for you," the student said.

"You walked 120 miles to give me this gift?" the teacher asked.

"Yes. The walk was part of the gift."

"Living in gratitude means that the act of giving is the gift itself."

— Mary Morrissey

When you think about gratitude as a state of mind instead of relying on something happening first to be grateful for, it takes it to a whole new level. When gratitude is your state of being, you align yourself with abundance. When it becomes a way of being, a way of living, that's harmony, and that's where deep joy lives.

"The roots of all goodness lie in the soil of appreciation for goodness."

— Dalai Lama

Being open to gratitude as a state of being is rooted in the concept of being open to receiving help, gifts of kindness, sincere compliments, and/ or recognition. It is as important to be a good giver as it is to be a good receiver. When you allow yourself to receive, you will always have things to be grateful for.

I learned the value of being open to receiving when I was caring for Marie. I was in the classic state of being a full-time family caregiver, which includes helping at all costs. It is in my nature to want to help others, but as a caregiver to a terminally ill patient, this need was multiplied a hundred times. However, I was never very comfortable asking for help myself. I kept thinking I could handle everything on my own. After all, Marie and her kids were counting on me.

One day, a woman called who said she was part of the Sunshine Committee at my daughter Christina's elementary school. I said I had never heard of the committee. She said that was because they stayed under the radar and helped families who were going through tough times. They had heard about our situation and knew how tough it was, so this woman was offering to bring over dinners from the Sunshine Committee as often as we would like.

I thought about how stubborn Marie was being about what she would eat. I thought it would be too much trouble for whoever was doing the cooking. Unbelievably, I said no thank you to the Sunshine Committee and their generous offer.

Please understand, right before Marie moved in, a burst water pipe had caused us to shut off some of the hot water in the house, which included the kitchen sink and the dishwasher. I had to wash dishes by hand in a bathtub. This with three extra people in the house and family from out of town dropping in periodically to visit Marie. On top of that, Christina came down with the swine flu. Keeping the house germ-free became my highest priority, which entailed washing dishes in the hottest water. How insane was I to decline the Sunshine Committee's help!

"You will be effortlessly filled with as much as you
can open yourself to receive."

— Bryant McGill

Tommy kept telling me I needed to get out at night with friends and just take a break from caregiving. I kept telling him I couldn't; Marie needed me. Finally, one day he put his hands on my shoulders, looked straight into my eyes, and said, "Patti, you've started to crack at the seams. Your patience is fraying. We have a seven-year-old daughter who is watching you and seeing you stressed. You need to get out." He promised he would take care of Marie, her kids, and Christina while I went out with my friends. Tommy pretty much had to push me out of the house as I tried to resist his help. When I did finally get out, I realized just how much I had needed the break. I was so grateful to him for persisting until I stopped resisting the gift he was trying to give me.

"Gracious acceptance is an art—an art which most never bother to
cultivate. We think that we have to learn how to give, but we forget about
accepting things, which can be much harder than giving…. Accepting
another person's gift is allowing them to express their feelings for you."

— Alexander McCall Smith

A couple of months before Marie died, she was starting to get out of bed in the middle of the night. On one occasion, I heard noises and got up to find her washing a sweater in the bathroom sink with water overflowing onto the floor. The next night, I found her turning on the gas stove burners. I declared to Tommy, "That's it. I'm sleeping downstairs on the couch where I can see what's happening in the middle of the night." After almost a week of me pretty much not sleeping, Tommy said, "You can't live like this. You're burning out and need help at least through the night so you can rest."

I resisted at first, but being so exhausted, I gave in, and we brought in a caregiver from 8 p.m. to 8 a.m. It truly saved me. And it helped everyone—Marie, my family, and me.

I learned allowing myself to receive help allowed me to give help more effectively. I was so grateful for all the help I was receiving and learned to graciously receive help with open arms and an open heart. I saw how gratitude truly serves the giver *and* the receiver.

> *"There are only two ways to live your life. One is as though nothing*
> *is a miracle. The other is as though everything is a miracle."*
>
> — Albert Einstein

I want to close this chapter with a special message of gratitude and appreciation to my husband and daughter. Thank you, Tommy and Christina, for your understanding, patience, compassion, and support. You gave so selflessly when Aunt Marie was ill and moved in with us so I could take care of her. Everything changed for our family, and that was a monumental sacrifice on your part. I am so deeply grateful to you both.

"Let us be grateful to people who make us happy; they are the charming gardeners who make our souls blossom."

— Marcel Proust

Take time to tap into your memory. Reflect on every experience and everyone who has touched your life. Focus on the feeling of gratitude, and let it be the lens you see and live your life through.

"Gratitude is the healthiest of all human emotions. The more you express gratitude for what you have, the more likely you will have even more to express gratitude for."

— Zig Ziglar

Inspired Insight:

_____

_____

_____

_____

Inspired Action:

Start a gratitude journal by writing down five things you're grateful for and read it every morning and night, adding one more thing each time. Do this for thirty days.

Do something nice for someone today—a loving act of kindness just because.

_____

_____

_____

_____

"Thankfulness is the beginning of gratitude. Gratitude is the completion of thankfulness. Thankfulness may consist merely of words. Gratitude is shown in acts."

— Henri Frederic Amiel

CHAPTER 12

7-UNITE WITH A NEW SELF-IMAGE

"Come out of the masses. Stand alone like a lion and live your life according to your own light."

— Rajneesh

W ho are you, really? At your core, what is most important to you and holds the most meaning? What are your deepest beliefs, the ones that shape your thoughts and consequently shape your life? When you think from your core, you tap into your authentic self. There you connect with your soul and live from your heart. It's where the magic happens. It's where you tap into joy and purpose. The key is embracing it as your identity within your self-image. It is the foundation from which you build your dreams and grow your vision of your what's next evolution.

"Every day you must try to make your own
self-image grow; this you can do."

— Maxwell Maltz

Maxwell Maltz was a plastic surgeon who figured out that how you see yourself dictates who you become. He said, "You can never outperform your own self-image." And that is because, as he discovered, we all have a mental blueprint in our subconscious where our beliefs, habits, and patterns live. Now you may not be able to outperform your own self-image, but the good news is you can certainly change it. This is about stepping into "I am." It means owning it. And you own it by becoming it.

"A human being always acts and feels and performs in accordance with
what they imagine to be true about them and their environment."

— Maxwell Maltz

Think again about how you started out as a youngster, fascinated with the abundant possibility that life had to reveal to you in your play journey. You asked yourself with a carefree open mind, "Who do I want to be today?" And then you zipped yourself up into that role. You stepped into who you wanted to be and had fun making it up as you went along. The key is you stepped into that role; you became that character. You weren't attached to a particular outcome, other than enjoying it and seeing where it would take you, allowing yourself the freedom to explore and experience without inhibitions.

"Step all the way in. Don't just put a foot in the door of your own life."

— Christine E. Szymanski

Look at creating your new self-image like creating your life's script.

Since we have many chapters in our lives, I like to say we have many lead roles to play in our life's script. But we must put that lead role on by becoming the character in our script. This is where role models can help.

Think about people you admire. Maybe someone is doing work you admire, someone has a relationship you admire, or someone lives a healthy lifestyle you admire. Look at what they are doing differently than you in the particular area you admire and would love for yourself. What do they say yes to and what do they say no to? What time do they start their day? What do they eat, and how do they keep healthy? What do they read? How do they spend their free time? Whom do they surround themselves with? Then look at your own habits to see how they align. This process is what actors do when they're stepping into their next role. They study the character in as much detail as they can until they become the character. It's about aligning with what you aspire to become, which will require you to step into a new self-image.

"Life is a lively process of becoming."

— Douglas MacArthur

Until I ran the Los Angeles Marathon, I never thought of myself as a marathon runner. It started out as an idea in conversation. Then I became more curious and ignited, which eventually turned into an actual desire to run the marathon. I had to put that role on. To become a marathon runner, I asked myself what action step I needed to take. My answer was I needed to start training like a marathon runner. I asked for help from someone who had run marathons, and they told me what I needed to do to prepare. I listened, and I did what they said. Through discipline and effort, I ran the marathon, which was a great accomplishment. But more than that, I actually became a marathon runner and had the habits of a marathon runner.

"Our self-image and our habits tend to go together. Change
one and you will automatically change the other."

— Maxwell Maltz

Think about all your habits. Some may be serving you better than others. If you don't like the results you're getting, do an honest assessment of yourself. What is your perception of how you see yourself in a given part of your life? What is success for you in this particular area? Replace any negative or limiting perceptions with positive ones that will truly serve your goals and dreams. When you make this change, you will look at yourself in a different way, and your entire world will begin to change.

What others think doesn't matter. But it's absolutely crucial to see yourself and feel yourself as the successful person in a relationship you love, doing work you love, earning an income you love, experiencing physical health you love, and living a life you love. When you get up in the morning, put on your new self-image. See yourself as the person who is the next best version of you. And adopt habits that align with your new self.

> *"To change a habit, make a conscious decision;*
> *then act out the new behavior."*
>
> — Maxwell Maltz

The only way to change a habit is to replace it with a new behavior. And to make it stick as a way of *being*, focus and repetition are required. Our dreams are for stretching us, and part of that process is seeing our dreams for ourselves.

Perception plays an important role in forming your self-image.

Understand that you always have a choice as to how you want to see yourself and what you want to believe about yourself. You are powerful and in control of your life. Therefore, you can change anything that isn't serving your growth and your what's next evolution. But when you keep this power to choose locked up inside you, you remain stuck. Think of your what's next evolution as an ongoing thing.

You should always be updating your self-image. It's like when you were growing up and continued to grow out of your clothes. You had to replace the old clothes that didn't fit anymore with new clothes you grew into. As we evolve into a newer version of ourselves, an improved version, it requires us to study and learn some new things, which brings us new awareness on a higher level, at a higher frequency.

"The minute that we change our minds, and stop giving power
to the past, the past with its mistakes loses power over us."

— Maxwell Maltz

I deeply believe we're never too old to step into a new role. If we're breathing, we should be evolving at some level. Sure, change and growth can be uncomfortable and daunting, but it's in our nature to continuously grow. Otherwise, we stagnate. Mary Morrissey put it well when she said, "Every day is like a lifetime in miniature. It has a beginning, and it has an end. You get to shape it."

"Look around you. Everything changes. Everything on this earth is in a continuous state of evolving, refining, improving, adapting, enhancing, and changing. You were not put on this earth to remain stagnant."

—Steve Maraboli

When my mother passed away, my father was truly heartbroken. My younger sister Carrie and I really didn't think he'd last very long. Though he was in pretty good health, he had been caring for Mom, who had early-stage dementia, the last two years of her life. One day, everything changed. Mom suddenly slipped into late-stage dementia, and within three weeks, she died. And three weeks after Mom's death, our oldest brother Jim's daughter was killed in a tragic accident. At that point, we really didn't think Dad would make it through all the tragedy. He was so worn out from caregiving—physically, mentally, and emotionally.

What happened two months later was truly remarkable. Dad called me one day and said, "Patti, I've made a decision. I can either continue to look at these walls and wait to die or do something different. So, I've decided to reinvent myself." My dad was eighty-seven at the time.

I don't know that Dad really knew what it meant for him in the moment, but what he did know was he needed to move forward. Devastated as he was, he was still breathing. So, as he says, "I've got to keep moving." And he did.

Dad took an interest in learning to cook—he got curious. This is a man who in his retirement redid his basement (which looks like a home) and built a beautiful oak bar from scratch. What's funny is that this same man who used to love walking around Home Depot for inspiration was now sharing recipes with Carrie and me, and buying items from the kitchenware company Sur La Table was his new pleasure. Mom would not have believed it. Dad's new role—a man who cooks.

At this point in his life, when many of his friends had passed or were in poor health, Dad found himself very lonely. Mom was always the activity planner, so he found himself in uncharted and uncomfortable territory. Since the church was their nucleus for social gatherings and events, he started helping out there more. And he got involved in helping out some of his friends who were not in great shape. He told me he believed that was his new purpose—giving a helping hand. A new role and another self-image update.

My dad is now ninety-three and doing quite well. He told me about two recent trips to two separate doctors. He had a similar experience in both instances. When he got to the office and they put him in a room, the nurse and the office manager came in and asked him his name and birthdate. They thought they had the wrong file since he didn't act like a nonagenarian (a person in their nineties).

Sure, Dad's definitely slowed down and has his aches and pains. He's had prostate cancer and heart disease, but his attitude to keep moving forward continues to serve him. He's always looking for a new way to stay active and relevant. One of his grandchildren loves a Ukrainian version of sauerkraut called *kapusta*. You grate the cabbage and ferment it in a big wooden barrel—it's quite a process. Dad spent a Saturday with his grandson teaching him how to make it, barrel and all. You're never too old to teach. Another new role—mentor.

It's been so inspiring watching my dad evolve in this late stage of his life. His continuing to grow has helped him stay relevant at the ripe age of ninety-three. You get to choose for yourself every day to step into your I am role with an updated self-image.

> *"Every day, you reinvent yourself. You're always in motion.*
> *But you decide every day: forward or backward."*
>
> — James Altucher

We were designed to evolve and grow continuously—explore, discover, and become. But we must first claim it by stepping into it. Tell yourself, "I am the person claiming my next role as…. And this is what it looks like as I allow myself to embrace it, study it, practice it, and before I know it, I will have become it—an updated version of myself." The alternative is to stagnate, and allow life to have less and less meaning. It is always your choice. It is your responsibility to move yourself forward. No one can choose it for you. Open your imagination as you claim your next role on life's stage.

Now that you've been introduced to the IgniteU System, you've been empowered with seven simple strategies to help you navigate the unknown on the life path that eagerly awaits you so you can ignite what's next for you.

With an inspired vision, a clarity of solid goals, a strong why, a committed decision, the support of true partners in believing, and coming from the lens of deep gratitude while emboldened with a new updated self-image, you're now ready for Part III of this book. There you will learn how to break through the mind blocks that keep you stuck by reframing those limiting beliefs to lift you up and align you with a vision-driven life.

"I am prepared to evolve. The question is, are you?"

— Mother Nature

Inspired Insight:

Inspired Action:

Reflect on your dream, and think about how you will grow your self-image into the next best version. What new habits do you need to embrace, and which ones do you need to release? What's your new role on your life's stage?

_____

_____

_____

_____

"If you want to have more, you have to become more. Success is not something you pursue. Success is something you attract by the person you become. For things to improve, you have to improve. For things to get better, you have to get better. For things to change, you have to change. When you change, everything changes for you."

— Jim Rohn

PART III

BREAKING THROUGH MIND BLOCKS AND ALIGNING WITH A VISION- DRIVEN LIFE

?

CHAPTER 13

DESERVING A LIFE THAT INSPIRES YOU

"It was when I stopped searching for home within others and lifted the foundations of home within myself I found there were no roots more intimate than those between mind and body that have decided to be whole."

— Rupi Kaur

The power of possibility is limitless, and so are our capabilities to continue to evolve and grow into the next best version of ourselves. A baby doesn't stay an infant, a toddler doesn't keep crawling, nor does an awkward teenager remain in puberty. And so it goes as we continue to grow into the individuals we decide to let ourselves become.

You have the power to choose how you will direct your life. You've been given the capacity to choose what you think about, what feelings you attach to thoughts, and which actions you take with respect to those thoughts and feelings.

Your life journey is about constant discovery—discovering and learning things that will challenge you right up to your green growing edge and push you way outside your comfort zone. That's where you spread your wings, connect with your heart, and continue to evolve as the individual being you were created to be. It is where you unite with your authentic self, your soul. And it is where you align with your deep desire and purpose.

It starts with the belief that you deserve to have dreams and then continues when you give yourself permission to pursue those dreams. Otherwise, you create a feeling that you are undeserving, which causes resistance to positive change.

> *"You'll be amazed at what you attract after you start believing in what you deserve."*
>
> — Oui We

Now you have at least the beginnings of a dream, a vision, a possibility of what might be next. You've found something that lights you up and gets your adrenaline flowing, something with deep meaning for you that aligns with what you believe at your core. You've opened your imagination and allowed yourself to truly lean into limitless possibility. You've committed to moving forward with your what's next. It's exciting and exhilarating.

But now, lurking around the corner, hanging out on the edges of your possibility and waiting to grab hold of your attention and focus, are your doubts and limiting beliefs. Your current beliefs will question your abilities and worthiness to fulfill this beautiful, big vision. You've allowed yourself to dip your toe into the unknown, which is inspiring and motivating, new and different from anything you've known before. But it's not the you that you're familiar with, nor is it the you familiar to those who know you.

At this point, we usually feel the need to retreat. We quickly shrug off the new possibility and go right back to our comfort zone—whether it's pleasant or unpleasant, it's predictable. And before we know it, other people's opinions and fears take over as the authorities on what's best for us.

The bright light inside that once inspired us and fed our soul is replaced with a dimmer switch leading us to be more sensible and practical. It's safe and familiar. But the familiar us produces familiar results—no growth, no movement forward.

You can break free if you allow yourself to step into the next best version of you. And that starts with believing you are worthy and deserving of it.

> *"The only thing that keeps you from deserving or loving yourself or whatever, is someone else's belief or opinion that you have accepted as truth."*
>
> — Louise Hay

You were brought into creation with gifts to share and express in this world. Your life is seeking a freer and fuller expression by means of you. That's why you have an imagination and ideas that are beyond what you've experienced. They give you something to aim at, a big bodacious goal that fires you up inside. Your dream is your compass pointing you in the direction of your what's next.

Self-help author and lecturer Bob Proctor used to say, "Goals aren't for getting; they're for growing." It starts out as an idea, a dream, a vision of what could be, and then it is up to you to take inspired action toward the dream. Find a vision that lights you up and inspires you every day to want to continue to move toward making your possibilities into your reality. Trust your inner voice instead of looking outside for approval. It's about leaning into your truth rather than just the facts. The facts may be that you're in a job you don't love, you're in a ho-hum relationship, you're in debt, you've been diagnosed with a disease, you're too thin or overweight, or you're working in a toxic environment—but whatever the actual facts may be, they don't have to be your truth unless you believe them to be true.

Because the truth is a Higher Power exists in the universe that is bigger than anything you may be experiencing right now. You are more capable than you know, and you have a power in you bigger than anything outside of you. You've been given these beautiful capacities, the gifts of imagination and intuition, to guide you on your what's next path if you are open to it. Allow yourself the freedom to dream and trust your inner voice to follow what's lighting up your soul, begging you to explore and ignite what's next for you.

"No matter how qualified or deserving we are, we will never reach a better life until we can imagine it for ourselves and allow ourselves to have it."

— Richard Bach

Though I enjoyed my creative writing class my sophomore year of high school, I never thought of myself as an author. As I mentioned earlier, I didn't even really like to read until I discovered personal development articles and books in my late teens and early twenties. So, when the idea of writing a book came up, I tried to dismiss it altogether. And when I mentioned it to Tommy, he said, "Oh, now you're going to become an author? What do you know about writing a book?"

I understood why he might say that since I thought the same thing at first. Tommy has always been supportive of my endeavors, even when some of them didn't work out as I had hoped. I got that he saw this as another new thing I was pursuing and a distraction from building my coaching business. But I couldn't shake the idea, and it became a burning desire. I saw it as a thread weaving into my coaching programs and the foundation from which to build my business mission.

I first thought about just publishing a short ebook. I mentioned it to a friend who had successfully published a book herself a few years back. She encouraged me to speak with her book coach, Patrick. After she nudged me (accountability and support) by doing an email introduction, I reluctantly decided to at least make the call—an inspired action step. I explained that I loved coaching and speaking in front of professional groups and organizations. He simply said, "Write a full-length paper book instead of a short ebook."

I told Patrick I didn't think I could do that since I was no author (limiting belief). He said he understood why I might think that, but he believed differently (supportive partner in believing). He gave me some homework to do, regardless of what I decided. Basically, he broke down very simply how to create an outline. I decided to give it a try (inspired action), and that's when my aha moment hit me. When I drafted the beginnings of an outline, which then became the chapters in my book, is when I started to believe I could actually write a book. That awareness opened me up to the belief that I deserved to do it because it was important to me and it could also help others.

What I didn't realize when I started writing this book was how much it would cause me to reflect on my own life journey. What a powerful process and experience writing has been. It has given me the opportunity to look back at my successes, failures, and lessons. I was able to see all the dots connecting to bring me to where I am today. It truly helped me believe in the big dreams that might still be ahead for me.

> *"Too many people overvalue what they are*
> *not and undervalue what they are."*

— Malcom Forbes

Women of my mom's generation didn't have the opportunities my generation and future generations have. Back then, it was commonly thought a mother would be selfish if she went after a dream. What often happened was family came first, second, and third, and somehow mothers always ended up left in the dust with unfulfilled dreams.

> *"Consider the fact that maybe…just maybe…beauty and*
> *worth aren't found in a makeup bottle, or a salon-fresh*
> *hairstyle, or a fabulous outfit. Maybe our sparkle comes from*
> *somewhere deeper inside, somewhere so pure and authentic*
> *and real, it doesn't need gloss or polish or glitter to shine."*

— Mandy Hale

Near the end of the movie *Dirty Dancing*, Baby, played by Jennifer Grey, is sitting in the corner at a table with her family. Johnny, played by Patrick Swayze, comes over, scoops her onto her feet, and says to the family, "Nobody puts Baby in a corner." That moment of truth drove home the point that Baby deserved to be in the spotlight of her own life and dreams.

And she shined on that dance floor, displaying beauty and grace as the authentic being she desired to experience and become—and with the man of her dreams.

We are all deserving of our visions and dreams. But it is up to us to discover and realize them. It starts with truly believing we are worthy and deserve to live a life that inspires us, a life filled with passion, meaning, and purpose.

> *"Nobody needs to prove to anybody what they're worthy of, just the person that they look at in the mirror. That's the only person you need to answer to."*
>
> — Picabo Street

If you're still wondering if you're worthy and deserving, be assured you are.

We've all been given these beautiful capacities and the ability to choose what's next for us. It's really our responsibility to continue to grow and evolve. It's how we were designed to live. We are deserving of our dreams and possibilities, but we must decide to claim them.

Allow yourself to fuse with the very belief that, as a child of this infinite universe, you are absolutely deserving of a life that fills you with joy and purpose.

"Never limit yourself because of others' limited imagination; never limit others because of your own limited imagination."

— Mae Jemison

Inspired Insight:

_____

_____

_____

_____

Inspired Action:

_____

_____

_____

_____

"You alone are the judge of your worth and your goal is to discover infinite worth in yourself, no matter what anyone else thinks."

— Deepak Chopra

CHAPTER 14

TRUSTING YOUR INTUITION

"Follow your instincts. That's where true wisdom manifests itself."

— Oprah Winfrey

I t is important to trust yourself first. And yet many people don't, and without knowing, they block their superpower—intuition. Yes, it's actually a superpower, and it is one of the mental faculties you were born with. You were given six extraordinary gifts—intuition, imagination, will, memory, reason, and perception. These mental faculties—your superpowers—give you the ability to transform your life. Yet most of us live more by our five senses—what we can see, hear, taste, smell, and touch. And we interpret the world through our senses, and then live our lives based on our conditions. It's crazy, though, because we were not built to live through outside conditions.

"Intuition is the compass of the soul."

— Anonymous

You were designed to live authentically from the inside out. You were given a brilliant internal guidance system, which is your intuitive faculty, that gut feeling, what some call the inner voice. Your intuition isn't outside of you; it's within you. Your life is an inner journey of self-discovery. Part of that is learning to trust your inner self. And to do that, you need to quiet your mind and calm your physical system. In tranquility and quiet, you can hear the still small voice. This is the true purpose of meditation. It calms your mind and body; it's about relaxation. Meditation is about turning off the outside world so you can look inward and tune into what your soul is saying to you.

My oldest brother Jim made a decision based strictly on intuition that ultimately changed his life. The COVID-19 pandemic shut down the world in March 2020. Jim was supposed to go in for a colonoscopy but decided to put it off until things settled down a bit. In June, he felt an inner nudge to schedule it. Even his wife thought it might be better to wait a bit longer, but his gut was urging him to move forward. Jim made the choice to listen to his inner voice, trust his gut feeling, and schedule the colonoscopy. Mind you, he was feeling fine at the time.

"Intuition is reason in a hurry."

— Holbrook Jackson

When the results came back, Jim was shocked. He had colon cancer. The doctor wanted to scan the organs around Jim's colon before operating to remove the cancer just to be sure it hadn't spread. He said it was routine, and he didn't think it had spread. They found a spot on Jim's liver. He had stage four cancer.

Though this diagnosis was serious, the doctor believed with aggressive radiation and chemotherapy Jim could recover fully. It definitely wasn't easy since Jim had every adverse reaction to the chemo a person could have—it caused heart attack-like symptoms twice, paper cut sores all over his fingers, welts on his face and mid-section, and other typical chemo side effects.

After a short cancer-free period, Jim's cancer came back. But thankfully, he's in remission right now. If he had dismissed his gut feeling—his inner voice or intuition—Jim's outcome could have been very different. It was reasonable to put it off since he had no symptoms and we were in the middle of a worldwide pandemic, but his inner self knew better and warned him. And Jim listened. And he trusted himself. He made his decision based on what felt right to his intuition.

"Intuition doesn't tell you what you want to hear;
it tells you what you need to hear."

— Sonia Choquette

The same is true with your big dreams—your inner voice speaks from your soul and is the core of who you truly are. When you're asking, "What's next for me?", you want to pay close attention to what's going on inside you. Trust whatever that is and act. Plant the seeds of your dream and allow them to take root in the rich soil of your mind. Nurture those seeds and the soil by paying attention to the thoughts you fertilize your subconscious with. Trust the process by trusting the power that's breathes through you.

"Intuition is the whisper of the soul."

— Jiddu Krishnamurti

Steven Spielberg had some really good insight on this very thing:

The thing I really want to emphasize is, I didn't have a choice. I didn't have a choice...the dream is something you never knew was going to come into your life. Dreams always come from behind you, not right between your eyes. It sneaks up on you. But when you have a dream, it doesn't often come at you screaming in your face, "This is who you are, this is what you must be for the rest of your life." Sometimes a dream almost whispers. And I've always said to my kids, the hardest thing to listen to—your instincts, your human personal intuition— always whispers; it never shouts. Very hard to hear. So you have to every day of your lives be ready to hear what whispers in your ear; it very rarely shouts. And if you can listen to the whisper, and if it tickles your heart, and it's something you think you want to do for the rest of your life, then that is going to be what you do for the rest of your life, and we will benefit from everything you do.

I just knew deep in my soul that I needed to write this book as my what's next move. And yet partway through, I put it aside as I allowed outside influences of doubt to get inside, which resulted in procrastination. My inner voice persisted. But until I chose to listen to it, I kept feeling I was being held back from truly stepping into my next best version. One day I found myself giving advice to Christina about trusting her inner voice. It hit me what a poor role model I was being by putting off my book. I remembered why it was important to me and used that as fuel to charge back in and finish what I started. Today I'm a published author with a strong purpose and mission to help others ignite their what's next evolution and truly "be" the leaders of their own lives.

"Our intuition is like a muscle, we must practice listening to it and trusting its wisdom. When you take the time to ask and keep listening for the answer, being at peace becomes easy."

— Lisa Prosen

Life is especially challenging when we feel we can't find our way out of a problem or around a roadblock. Just as we were all built to continually grow and evolve, so we were built with all the answers to our most perplexing questions. Though more often than not, we tend to look for answers outside of ourselves. But who better to answer our questions then ourselves? We just need to learn how to access those answers.

Within you lives this powerful mental faculty called intuition. It is your personal GPS. It is the voice of truth within that speaks to you every day. It's where hunches, gut sense, inner voice, ideas, or dreams that quietly nudge you come from. But no real power comes from being aware of intuition and not acting upon it. This source of intelligence provides insight and wisdom to help guide you if you can relax and quiet yourself enough to connect with it. Listen and trust it enough to act on its guidance.

"It is through science that we prove, but through intuition that we discover."

— Henri Poincare

Thomas Edison is said to have rocked in his rocking chair to quiet his mind. He was so effective that he relaxed enough to doze off. To act as an alarm, he would hold a rock in his hand with a metal bucket under it, so when the rock fell, it would wake him up. That's how quiet and still he got as he thought deeply about solutions he was looking for. He was patient and fully present, aware of how the mind works. He focused on his desired outcome with the expectation, belief, and trust that answers would eventually come. And they did. And the whole world benefited from it.

"Trusting our intuition often saves us from disaster."

— Ann Wilson Schaef

Sometimes it's not a pressing question or problem that begs listening to your inner voice. Intuition is a crucial faculty when it comes to danger or when you get a "bad feeling" about a person or situation.

I'm sure you can recall a time when you felt something was not right. And in that moment, you had a choice to make: Do I decide to listen or dismiss?

I heard a remarkable story from the morning of 9/11. A man who regularly flew United Flight 93 to the West Coast was scheduled that day to be on that flight. He was actually already in his car and on his way to the airport when he got a gut feeling telling him to turn around and take a later flight. The nudge came from a bad feeling about missing an event at his son's school (or so he thought). He really wanted to be there for his son, so he decided he could fly out later that day and still fulfill his business obligation. That decision to listen significantly changed his and his family's lives. He trusted his still small voice. We're built with an internal GPS system, but we must pay close attention to the signs and signals.

"The voice of truth speaks to all of us every single day
and it's as loud as our willingness to listen."

— Mary Morrissey

As I said earlier, when I landed my dream job in fashion, it came down to an intuitive, quick decision to go straight to the interview instead of going home to change. Had I gone home first, I would have been near the end of the long line of women who showed up right after me, and it is likely someone else could have been a good fit and received the job offer. To this day, I remember that nudge telling me to turn left and go straight to the interview. I dismissed it at first and passed the street where I needed to turn. The nudge told me I was already so close to where the interview was, why drive thirty minutes to turn around and come back? I didn't overthink it and instead chose to trust and listen to the nudge, taking me straight to my destiny.

You just don't know what you don't know. One of the biggest lessons I learned as a young adult was to be open-minded to allow new opportunities in and trust my inner guidance system. This put me on a trajectory that led to an exciting and lucrative dream career that truly changed my life. Looking back, it's one of many examples of how opportunity is always around us in this abundant universe. But we must listen, pay attention, trust, and act—because action changes things!

"Think for yourself. Trust your own intuition.
Another's mind isn't walking your journey, you are."

— Scottie Waves

Inspired Insight:

_____

_____

_____

_____

Inspired Action:

_____

_____

_____

_____

"There is a universal intelligent life force that exists within everyone and everything. It resides within each one of us as a deep wisdom, an inner knowing. We can access this wonderful source of knowledge and wisdom through our intuition, an inner sense that tells us what feels right and true for us at any given moment."

— Shakti Gawain

CHAPTER 15

USING FEAR AS YOUR FUEL

"The quickest way to acquire self-confidence is to do
exactly what you are afraid to do."

— Anonymous

believe fear is misunderstood. It is an enormous power that can be directed in service of your growth. In most cases, fear is not something to run away from; instead, it can be very empowering if embraced.

First, what exactly is fear? It can be defined as a strong emotion caused by worry about something dangerous, painful, or unknown. Here, the imagination can run rampant if you're not paying attention. Fear can also give you courage. Just look at the polarity of fear. On the one hand, it can keep you stuck or take you down, resulting in weakness. On the other hand, it can fuel you with courage and help you move through deep pain, danger, or the unknown, resulting in strength. How you choose to perceive and actually use its power is up to you. You've been given the capability to think freely. And that's why understanding these two sides of fear is so important. You get to choose how you see something (what picture you imagine), what you make of it (the emotion you wrap around it), and how you will respond (what action you take). Let fear be the fuel that empowers you to move into your what's next.

FEAR can have two meanings:

- Forget Everything And Run
- Face Everything And Rise

The choice is yours.

Fear is not an emotion most people embrace. It's uncomfortable and can be very scary, even paralyzing.

Back in the early '90s, I was living in an apartment in Burbank, California. I came home one Sunday night from a weekend trip. I was in the bathroom when I felt a breeze from the bedroom just across the hall. I looked into my dark bedroom and noticed a light shining through the blinds, which were blowing back and forth.

Then I noticed shimmering particles all over my bed. I looked a bit closer and realized it was broken glass. I was alone and the first thing I thought was, "*Oh my God, someone broke into my apartment, and they might still be in here!*"

I felt a wave of fear and panic rush over me. I froze and thought, *Should I stay and look around, or do I run?*

For a brief moment, my feet would not move. My mind kept shifting—stay or go. I was paralyzed with fear. But when I focused, the answer hit me—possible danger equals get out right now—so I did.

I found the apartment manager, who said a kid had accidentally thrown a ball through my window earlier that day. They were going to fix it the next morning. I was happy that was all it was, but I was floored by how an emotion could have so much power over my body, enough to temporarily stop me from moving.

Even though the reality was it was just an accident, that wasn't obvious; therefore, I didn't feel safe in that moment. And although in fact there was no danger, my mind believed there was, and my body responded to what it believed to be true in that moment. As I took back my power by focusing and listening to my intuition, I was able to use my fear as fuel to help myself get moving again and get away from the potential danger.

> *"No power so effectually robs the mind of all its powers of acting and reasoning as fear."*
>
> — Edmund Burke

While fear can paralyze and terrorize, it also causes adrenaline to kick in, giving a person extraordinary strength. You've heard heroic stories of people who can suddenly lift a car to get their trapped child out from under it. Again, fear has the power to weaken and the power to strengthen. That's some potent energy at your disposal. The key is in how you choose to harness your fear.

In Kelly Clarkson's song "Strong," the main verse uses the old adage that what doesn't kill you, makes you stronger. Use your fear as your fuel and amazing things can happen. When my grandmother slipped in her basement and broke her hip, she was alone and scared, but she used her fear as fuel to get to the phone upstairs. Her adrenaline kicked in, firing up her determination and focus, allowing her to drag herself slowly up each stair, pulling herself up with her arms. My grandmother was a hearty woman, and it was no easy task, especially since she was in her nineties, but she made it to the phone. Then she had to let Dad in, but she managed. Again, she used fear as fuel.

When you hear the phrase "Be fearless," don't take it to mean there's no fear involved. Being fearless is about how you identify with fear and what you decide to do with it. You don't necessarily get rid of the fear, but you can learn to work with it by thinking of it as a useful asset. Fear can alert you by heightening your awareness and warning you about danger ahead. It can cause pain to alert you something is wrong in your body. It can also motivate and inspire your dream and help you accomplish anything you set your mind to. These are all sides to a very powerful tool. Yes, fear can be a tool if you allow it to help you rather than stop you. It's a matter of framing your fear so it serves and fuels your growth.

"Everything you want is on the other side of fear."

— Jack Canfield

When you learn to honor your fear and its presence, it will truly serve you. Mary Morrissey said, "People are successful in the presence of their fear, not in the absence of their fear." When Christina was very young, Tommy and I often took her to one of the many parks in our neighborhood. I noticed she was afraid of climbing up too high, and unconsciously, I said out loud that she was afraid of heights. Tommy asked me not to make it an issue. He was afraid of heights, but had always challenged himself to face his fear; he didn't let it stop him from doing things, including giving him some great experiences like parasailing and the thrill of riding roller coasters.

I started paying attention and quickly stopped myself in mid-sentence when I slipped up. And eventually, through awareness and repetition, I stopped mentioning it altogether. That was repatterning. And what a difference it made. Christina didn't shy away from heights, and by the time she was in middle school, she challenged herself to ride the biggest roller coasters at Magic Mountain and loved the thrill of them.

Having been a cautious kid myself, it was a pretty cool transformation to watch. And when we vacationed in Maui one summer, Christina decided she would paraglide and skipped the 1,000-foot jump to take on the 3,000-foot one. Off the mountain she went with her guide. Watching her up in the air and seeing the big smile on her face when she landed was priceless. Just like her dad, she did not allow her fear of heights to stop her; rather it fueled her, which opened up new adventures for her.

"Men are not afraid of things, but of how they view them."

— Epictetus

How we look at fear is what's important. It's a good idea to run from real danger. But truthfully, most of the time what we are afraid of is harmless, so we are not in any imminent danger. We fear the border of our lives, the edge of our comfort zone. We fear the green growing edge of possibility and the uncertainty that lives there.

But your dreams—your what's next—are on the other side of that border. That's the unknown that will always be outside of your comfort zone. Henry David Thoreau calls it the invisible boundary. The gap between where we are and where we want to be is where fear hangs out. Instead of letting it stop you, acknowledge it for what it is—a powerful tool to propel you to the next best version of yourself. It's required to get you over the chasm and into your what's next evolution.

This is why your dream, your big bodacious goal, is key. It's where you are focused every day. It's especially critical when you are afraid, when you're riding that green growing edge of the unknown and discomfort. Your dream gives you a place to focus; it's a reminder of what's most important to you. And when your fear knocks you off course, your dream serves as your lighthouse, the beacon that helps you get back on course and moving toward what lights you up and feeds your soul.

Know this—as soon as you step outside your comfort zone and open yourself up to possibility, fear will pop up along with your current paradigms. They're buddies and will show up as a distraction, a naysayer, or an unpleasant event that wants to give you an excuse to turn back. Your old paradigms, your old belief system, questions anything new and comes up with excuses for why it's not for you: I'm too old. I'm not strong enough. I'm not healthy enough. I'm not experienced enough. It's okay to have fear; you just don't want fear to have you.

> *"Without fear there cannot be courage."*
>
> — Christopher Paolini

Reframe your fear as the fuel to catapult you to your dream. View it as an asset. That's the perception to embrace. And when you understand that fear is required to move forward, you will no longer look at it in the same way. Fear will propel you through the gap between where you are now and where you would love to go—where you are meant to be. When you allow yourself to move through fear by embracing it and then using it to fuel your charge forward, it gives you courage.

And with courage comes confidence. When you are confident, you stop being a victim and take responsibility for the choices you make. If you don't like something, you change it. You realize that being happy comes down to the choices you make and what you are willing to do to create the life you want—even in the face of fear!

"Courage is resistance to fear, mastery of fear, not absence of fear."

— Mark Twain

Inspired Insight:

_____

_____

_____

_____

Inspired Action:

_____

_____

_____

_____

"Each of us must confront our own fears, must come face to face with them. How we handle our fears will determine where we go with the rest of our lives."

— Judy Blume

CHAPTER 16

REFRAMING FAILURE AS FEEDBACK

"Failure is a detour, not a dead-end street."

— Zig Ziglar

H ow you choose to see things is also pivotal in dealing with failure. When you fail at something, it can be devasting. But it should not define you. Understanding this perception shift is huge. Fear and failure don't have to break you. In fact, they are required to build you up by teaching and grounding you. In the previous chapter, I spoke about the various sides of fear and how we can use fear to fuel us rather than stop us. Learning to work with failure is similar. When you reframe failure to instruct you by stepping back and taking inventory, it allows you to learn something about yourself. What's most important with failure is learning how to process it. When you look at failure as constructive feedback that happens simply to guide you, it heightens your awareness. Sometimes failure is merely meant to be a slap in the face to wake you up to something bigger, or it might be needed to knock you on your butt to recenter you.

"Most people have attained their greatest success just
one step beyond their greatest failure."

— Napoleon Hill

Failure has a tremendous power just like fear. Failure has the power to take you down, leading to misery, depression, angst, frustration, sadness, guilt, and sometimes even death. It can turn your life upside down.

And yet, that's not what failure is intended to do. It is intended to instruct. It can be a powerful tool that, when properly understood, will move you forward and help you achieve incredible results, results that build your mental muscles, results that help you grow and become the person you were designed to be.

Failure is how you develop your gifts and talents. It is up to you to discover what those are and then use your gifts in the world. Using your gifts starts with experimenting with ideas and being curious, trying something new and different, leaning into what lights you up and stirs your imagination. Failure is necessary for growth but can be very difficult to process. When you take it personally and allow it to define you, it can be crushing. It can be embarrassing and humiliating. Worse yet, it can become an identity you put on and start to believe in, eventually becoming the lens you view yourself through. The decisions you make and the paths you choose are driven by that lens that says you are not good enough or you are undeserving. It's the lens of lack and limitation and will stunt your growth, not expand it.

"Sometimes you win, sometimes you learn."

— John Maxwell

Looking back, one of my failures comes to mind because it almost led me to settle, which I said I'd never do. Remember the healthcare job I took at a startup that led to me quickly being promoted to president, which I wrote about in Chapter 5? When I realized it was best to close the business, failure reared its ugly head. Even though it wasn't my business, here I was shutting it down. Though grateful to have rallied support that allowed me to close things down properly, I went down the road of despair by adopting and embracing the identity of failure. I thought I would settle for less after that. I had accomplished a lot in my career, and now in mid-life, I had my family to focus on. I felt I had peaked in terms of what I could contribute on a grander scale.

I remained grateful for everything, but what wasn't sitting well with me was the idea of settling for less. It was not who I was, yet it was exactly where I was. Sometimes life takes you by surprise, and that was the real lesson for me. It was not the failure itself that was bad, but what I did with the feedback from that failure. Honestly, at first I used it against myself rather than in service to my growth. I became a victim of my failure rather than looking at it as feedback, allowing it to instruct my what's next.

What eventually slapped me in the face was thinking about my daughter Christina. What kind of example was I being for her? I didn't like it. I also thought about my husband Tommy and how hard he worked for our family. I wanted to contribute enough so he could slow down. I also thought about my sister Marie and how she only had fifty years on this planet. Coming from a feeling of gratitude for every day we are given, I decided at my core I was not a person who settles.

And actually, none of us are designed to settle. We were all meant to be awesome and to do awesome things. To do that, we try stuff, experience new ideas, and yes, in doing so, we make mistakes and fail. Failure truly is our best teacher, and it's necessary to learn and grow.

When you reframe failure as simply feedback, you can move forward with the lesson and leave behind the self-sabotage. Instead of owning your fact (your failure), own your truth, which is that you have unlimited capacity. It is there for you to discover what you would love to do and to put that out into the world.

"Remember that failure is an event, not a person."

— Zig Ziglar

Price Pritchett, author of *You Squared*, wrote, "Unless you allow yourself to make mistakes, to fail, you will never have the opportunity to test the limits of what you are truly capable of accomplishing."

The key is to change your perception of failure so you see it as absolutely necessary to moving yourself forward. Use your failure, your circumstance, in a useful way. This is when and how you learn. You learn by doing. You grow by trying new things, failing, and allowing the lesson to guide you, and then taking what you've learned to your next experience.

"Failure is only the opportunity to begin again, only this time more wisely."

— Henry Ford

I saw international inspirational speaker Liz Murray speak at a business event a few years back. Her amazing story is an example of reframing failure and circumstance to completely change your life. She and her sister grew up in New York City with parents who were cocaine addicts. Her parents spent most of their money on drugs. Murray and her sister were neglected. They went without food and begged neighbors for handouts. They even resorted to eating toothpaste. Their parents sold their winter coats to get money for drugs. When she was ten, Murray's mother got AIDS and Murray helped care for her. She talked about her mom sharing her dreams with her, yes even her drug-addict mom had dreams. Her mom eventually died. Her father failed to pay the rent on their flat, so he moved to a homeless shelter. Her sister got a place on a friend's couch, which left Murray, at age sixteen, on her own and homeless.

Murray said when she looked at the pine box her mom was buried in, she thought all her mom's dreams were buried with her in that coffin. Then something shifted within her. Murray realized she would be on that same road if she didn't change how she was living. She decided to go back to high school at age seventeen and pledged to become a "straight A" student and complete her high school education in just two years. And because she had a burning desire to learn with the strong intention of making more of her life, she thrived in school—all the while being homeless.

Through her school, Murray visited Harvard University. Once she saw it, she truly believed Harvard was a goal within her reach. She didn't let her current condition, the fact of being homeless, define her. It wasn't her identity, the truth of how she saw herself; it became just her current circumstance. She created a new self-image, which was that of a Harvard student. She focused on her dream—the truth of who she was at her core—and took action through the lens of possibility. It opened up a whole new world for her—one that took her where no one would have believed she could go. Murray knew where she wanted to go, and she saw herself there. Did she know exactly how she was going to get there? Not quite. But she did what she could (finish high school), from where she was (homeless but capable), with what she had (a big goal and the will to do whatever it took).

When Murray heard *The New York Times* was offering a scholarship to a needy local student who had overcome obstacles, she took inspired action. Her story was compelling, and she won the scholarship. In fact, readers were so moved by her story that they donated an additional $200,000, which was enough for fifteen more scholarships. Talk about making a difference!

Murray said when she looks back on the burden her parents put on her, she's not angry or bitter. She knows they did the best they could given that they had a serious addiction that prevented them from doing more. She also realized her experiences, bad and good, were a part of her and her journey. And she learned from her experiences and made use of the lessons.

If Murray had let her circumstances (neglect and poverty) and her failures (dropping out of school) define her, she would not have changed her life. She is now married with two children and speaks all over. She wrote a book titled *Breaking Night*, and Lifetime made a movie of her story called, *From Homeless to Harvard: The Liz Murray Story*.

You always have the power to change the trajectory of your life. And you get to decide how to frame that journey.

"Failure isn't fatal, but failure to change might be."

— John Wooden

Inspired Insight:

_____

_____

_____

_____

Inspired Action:

_____

_____

_____

_____

"I've missed more than 9,000 shots in my career. I've lost almost 300 games. Twenty-six times I've been trusted to take the game winning shot and missed. I've failed over and over and over again in my life. And that is why I succeed."

— Michael Jordan

?

CHAPTER 17

WALKING OFF LIFE'S STAGE IS NOT AN OPTION

"Successful men and women keep moving.
They make mistakes, but they don't quit."

— Conrad Hilton

I n the last chapter, we discussed the importance of looking at our failures from a constructive and instructive point of view rather than letting missteps take us down a dark rabbit hole. We tend to give up when we allow our failures to demoralize us. When we settle for something as opposed to really going for the thing we find most meaningful, it can sometimes lead us into the dark abyss.

When I was in high school, I had a job at a clothing store. Our manager was getting married, and she said she was pretty sure about her decision to do so. I remember thinking, *Pretty sure?* She said it was the right time in her life and she cared about her fiancé. But when the time came, she had second thoughts. She wasn't sure about marrying this man, but she ultimately decided, since all the plans were set in motion, she'd just go along with the wedding. In other words, she settled. Consequently, the marriage didn't last long.

> *"Please don't settle. Not in a job you hate, not in a town where you don't feel at home, not with friendships that aren't real, and especially, especially not with love."*
>
> — Marisa Donnelly

In my opinion, settling is a form of giving up, especially when it comes to big life decisions. Why is it that people settle so often? For some, it might seem easier just to go along to get along. Others may feel they don't deserve more. And some may just feel they should be grateful for what they have, which is true. But that doesn't mean we should stop wanting more for ourselves. And we absolutely do deserve more.

I'm saying this from the perspective of supporting continual evolution and growth. Why aren't we always striving for more, striving to be great? Good is the enemy of great. Great isn't about striving to be perfect, but about not accepting mediocrity and not giving up when things get challenging.

Sometimes we need to make a move and release something that isn't serving our growth. That's not giving up; that's letting go of what isn't serving our next best step and moving on by replacing it with something that is. It might be a new thought or a new action or even a new perspective.

When you decide to go in a different direction with the motivation to continue on your what's next evolution, you're not giving up; you're making a new decision that serves the next best version of yourself—an update for your self-image.

"There is no passion to be found in settling for a life that is less than the one you are capable of living."

— Nelson Mandela

I think of giving up as walking off life's stage before finishing the scene. If you quit before you've allowed yourself to see what you can do, your possibilities will be limiting. And if you've made a commitment to yourself or someone else, it's equally important to see it through and not quit on yourself or your commitment. First and foremost, it's important to honor your commitments because it's your word and you want to be impeccable with your word as renowned spiritual teacher and internationally bestselling author Don Miguel Ruiz points out in *The Four Agreements.* He says your word is a force in itself and a powerful tool. It can create or destroy.

So be mindful how you use your words both when talking to others and when talking to yourself. Self-talk is powerful because it directs your subconscious, which becomes your belief and ultimately dictates whom you become.

In my preteens, I was a Girl Scout. I loved it the first few years—all the activities and camping trips. But after a while, mid-membership year, I told my mom I wanted to quit. It just wasn't my thing anymore. She suggested I rethink "quitting." She encouraged me to stick to my commitment until the end of the year. She told me if I quit in the middle of the year, it would become that much easier to quit something the next time. And before long, being a quitter would become a habit, a way of being. I fought her on it at first, but the idea of going back on my word and being a quitter just didn't feel right. I weathered the rest of the year. The lesson I learned was huge—I didn't want to become good at quitting. I didn't want it to become my way of being. I didn't want to take on the identity of someone who knows how to quit. Giving up and quitting become habits.

> *"If you quit once, it becomes a habit. Never quit!"*
>
> — Michael Jordan

You can always choose the victim's journey or the hero's journey. The difference between the two is how you frame each experience. The victim's journey is one of blame and excuses. It is based on how life is happening "to me." The hero's journey is one of transforming circumstances into empowerments. It's about life happening "through me" as you learn through the challenges that confront you. It's based on taking what you've learned and experienced and using it to serve you.

Sports is full of comeback stories. To have a comeback, you have to be falling short of your goal. When you are losing, mindset, determination, and focus come into play big time. You can decide to put in your best effort and be open to the idea that anything is possible. If you allow yourself to believe you are far more capable than you know, then anything can happen.

"Defeat is not bitter unless you swallow it."

— Joe Clark

In September 2017, Tommy and I and some friends went to the UCLA versus Texas A&M football game at the Rose Bowl in Pasadena, California. Well into the third quarter, UCLA was losing painfully forty-four to ten. The facts were there were nineteen minutes to go, and UCLA was down by thirty-four points. Fans started leaving the stadium.

Tommy said, "Only five touchdowns, that's all we need."

UCLA needed a huge momentum change, but that didn't seem likely.

And then UCLA scored a touchdown.

And then a second and a third and then a fourth.

It was insane!

Something shifted within the team. First and foremost, they didn't give up. Even with their fans leaving and giving up on them, they didn't give up on themselves. And with two minutes and thirty-nine seconds to go, they scored a fifth touchdown and won the game forty-five to forty-four. Watching and feeling the momentum shift in the stadium was truly remarkable.

Mindset can make or break an opportunity. But you must first be able to see your challenge as an opportunity to remain focused on your desired result. If you see defeat, you are pretty much guaranteed defeat. But if you see the possibility, dig in with a new idea, and put in the effort, anything is truly possible.

> *"Character consists of what you do on the third and fourth tries."*
>
> — James A. Michener

From the moment I met Sarah, I knew there was something special about her, something I don't think she even yet saw in herself.

As part of the women entrepreneurs group, the eWomen Network, a few years ago I was on the committee to pick the Calabasas chapter's Emerging Leader award winner. We were looking for a young woman entrepreneur under thirty with a current business in the area. We interviewed three young women. When Sarah came in, she told us that on her way to the interview, she saw some little girls with a lemonade stand and had to stop to support their cause and give them kudos for being promising future women entrepreneurs.

Sarah then told her own story about the experience and lessons she had already learned in her hospitality career. She sounded like someone twice her age. She had lost all she had in a business venture with an associate who betrayed her. Instead of giving up and going back to her old job, she moved back home and started a dessert business with six dollars and a kitchen oven.

When Sarah left the interview, my colleagues and I unanimously agreed she would be our Emerging Leader. Her resilience, energy, drive, perseverance, and heart inspired us all. We collectively and intuitively felt she was on her way to success. She'd even started a charitable foundation of her own.

The Emerging Leader Award included attending our annual conference in Dallas and a fully paid one-year membership in our eWomen Chapter (age range primarily between forty and sixty-plus). Sarah later told us her friends teased her about spending so much time with "those old ladies." Jokes on them. We were wise, experienced, and connected. Sarah was fully engaged with our network, participating every month, and her business continued to expand because of it. The connections she made were invaluable, helping her hit the six-figure mark with her small business and pursue new aspirations to grow into a bigger hospitality venture.

And then COVID-19 hit, and the pandemic shut down the world. Most of Sarah's business was weddings and events. The wedding industry screeched to a halt, with bookings being put off indefinitely or canceled altogether.

At the same time, Sarah's grandfather, whom she was very close with, died. It was a very dark time for her. But while she was still processing everything, she managed to pick herself up. Rather than giving up as her circumstances tested her, she did something to help change her energy. She decided to bake for local nurses and essential workers, giving back with sweet treats from the heart. Rather than giving up, she focused on doing what she could from where she was with what she had.

> *"I have found that among its other benefits,*
> *giving liberates the soul of the giver."*
>
> — Maya Angelou

Also, just as the pandemic was closing the world down, Sarah was in the thick of raising money for a hospitality venture— her Dream Home and Celebration House in Nashville—and only had a short window of time left (what unfortunate timing). She doubled down (with a clear goal, focus, and strong why), and remarkably, successfully hit her target funding before the deadline. As the pandemic continued with no end in sight and more cancellations and postponements, Sarah made the painful decision to close the dessert part of her business, which was her main business, and focus on the hospitality side. It was a big risk, but it was her ultimate dream, and she was not going to settle or give up.

In early 2022, Sarah completed her beautiful Dream Home and Celebration House in Nashville. It looked just like the inspirational vision board she had showed us at our eWomen Conference when it was just the seed of an inspired idea in her imagination. This is how dreams are made.

There is so much more to Sarah's story, with so many silver linings to ongoing challenges, but the point is she never gives up on herself and her vision. Sarah is launching into her what's next evolution on a much larger scale as she continues to weather storms—while never walking off her life's stage. And because she has stuck with it, she finds opportunities she never could have imagined. She's now on a path to hit the seven-figure mark. And to put the cherry on top of all of this, she just got engaged to a great guy she met through her wise and seasoned networks.

Just think if she had given up on her dream and walked off her life's stage....

"The strongest people I've met have not been given an easier life. They've learned to create strength and happiness from dark places."

— Kristen Butler

We don't know how long we have on earth. But every day we wake up is a day full of possibility. And even in the dark storm of disease, we have the choice to give up or make something happen from where we are, with what we have.

I watched my sister Marie walk this journey. Between fighting cancer and going through a bitter divorce, she had many valid reasons not to finish school at UCLA. Often when she was going through chemo and radiation, I couldn't believe she wanted to continue her studies. But she absolutely refused to give up on what she really wanted. Looking back, I believe that along with her kids, going to school gave her a purpose and a positive place on which to focus.

I will always remember the day Marie received her degree as a landscape architect from UCLA. It was not only a proud moment, but profoundly inspirational—sending a clear message about not giving up on yourself when things get tough. Marie showed us when you focus on what you want and let it be your compass, a place to direct your attention and energy, you can accomplish more than you think possible.

"When the unthinkable happens, the lighthouse is hope.
Once we choose hope, everything is possible."

— Christopher Reeve

I met Chris when her hair was growing back after chemotherapy. Our husbands met at the tennis club, and we met up for dinner periodically. Chris had battled ovarian cancer and was just finishing treatment. This cancer is generally caught late, and when it comes back for a second time, it's usually a death sentence. Well, that's what happened with Chris, and the prognosis wasn't good. Tommy and I visited her in the hospital, thinking she didn't have much time. Chris ended up making it back home where she made a big decision. She was going to do absolutely everything in her power to fight this and not give up.

Chris knew her immune system was shot and any toxins could kill her. She started with her bathroom and went through every product, reading through the ingredients. She threw so much away. She said she started crying, realizing just how much crap was in so many of the products we use. Sure, with a strong immune system, a lot of this stuff can be pretty benign, but not hers, which was compromised because of her cancer. She ended up going through her entire home and then started to do research.

Chris found healthy products to replace the unhealthy ones. The process was arduous, but she looked at it as fighting for her life. Chris had the mercury fillings in her teeth removed. She found natural makeup and her face literally glowed with radiance. The doctors were amazed when she went into remission. For years, they wouldn't pull her chemo port out of her chest because they didn't believe the remission would last. Well, it's been almost two decades, and she's written a book, *Beating Ovarian Cancer* and is the Executive Director of the Ovarian Cancer Coalition of Greater California. Chris continues to live as clean a life as she can. She didn't walk off her life's stage even when her conditions and medical team (her facts) told her otherwise. She made a committed decision to fight for her life. She didn't give up on herself. You don't know what's possible until you try.

> *"Survival can be summed up in three words…*
> *never give up.*
> *That's the heart of it, really. Just keep trying."*
>
> — Bear Grylls

I'm so inspired by people who just keep trying no matter what they face. What's most important is avoid letting things define you. You are in the driver's seat of your life. Ultimately, you control your life by how you decide to think about it, feel about it, and live it. Yes, struggle, trauma, challenge, heartbreak, disease, or some other adversity will constantly present itself along your journey.

But you and I have been given free will; therefore, we have the freedom to choose what we make of any circumstance and how we navigate the conditions that confront us.

You are the director, producer, and actor on your life's stage. Don't let the audience write your lines. Remember, our big goals aren't so much for getting but for growing.

Don't settle or give up on your dreams because you'll be giving up on yourself, and that's not what you were designed to do.

Except us humans, all creatures are completely comfortable and oriented in their environment. They blend in. We don't because we've been given these magnificent and powerful capacities to create our own environment. Our life's journey is about trying new things, falling down, failing, getting up, and trying some more—we keep moving forward until we take our last breath. We are meant to believe in ourselves, and our journey is meant to manifest our what's next evolution!

> *"Maybe life isn't about avoiding the bruises. Maybe it's about collecting the scars to prove that we showed up for it."*
>
> — Hannah Brencher

Inspired Insight:

_____

_____

_____

_____

Inspired Action:

_____

_____

_____

_____

"When you have exhausted all possibilities, remember this: you haven't."

— Thomas Edison

CHAPTER 18

BELIEVING IN YOURSELF

"Confidence is the most beautiful thing you can possess."

— Sabrina Carpenter

I f you want other people to believe in you, you have to believe in yourself and wear that belief for everyone to see. You need to *be you*. How others see you really is up to you. To achieve your goals, you have to focus and put in maximum effort. If you don't believe in yourself, you won't give your full effort, and your chances of achieving your goals will be slim to none. Ultimately, your life is built by you or destroyed by you. Even when circumstances beyond your control present challenges, how you respond is always up to you. Will *you be* the hero of your life's movie and use challenges to empower you to learn something new about yourself?

"Self-trust is the first secret of success."

— Ralph Waldo Emerson

With one thing leading to another, it's easy to end up living life by default. How do you take back your power? First, let go of excuses, every single one of them. Sandra Yancey, CEO of eWomen Network, said, "When you lose your excuses, you find your results."

I met an amazing woman at an eWomen Network conference in Dallas, Texas, named Maggie Cook. Her story was truly riveting. She grew up in the mountains of central Mexico where her parents were missionaries caring for 200 abandoned and abused children in an orphanage. She was raised in poverty and saw so much trauma. She would retreat over a hill where she carved out a hole, which was the space where she could be alone with her thoughts and dreams. Cook said she would imagine herself wearing a suit as a businesswoman (updated self-image).

Cook was also a good basketball player, and when she graduated from high school, she was recruited to play for the Mexican National team. Unfortunately, before she got there, she broke her collarbone. Her father told her that her dreams were over. Though she was deeply disappointed, she refused to believe that and decided to believe something better than basketball was going to happen for her. That's believing in yourself even when others may not, even when your outside conditions seem dire.

"Believing in yourself doesn't make success easy. It makes success possible."

— Vickie L. Milazzo

Cook decided to continue to believe in herself. And as she did, another opportunity presented itself. She went to the United States with her family, looking for support for their nonprofit organization. While at a picnic in Charleston, West Virginia, the University of Charleston's women's basketball coach saw Cook playing basketball with her brothers from the orphanage. The coach offered her a scholarship. She graciously accepted it and moved to West Virginia. It was a wonderful opportunity, but Cook barely spoke English, so it was also very challenging in the beginning.

While at school, Cook made fresh salsa for her friends. They loved it and talked her into entering a salsa competition in West Virginia. She won $800 and used it to start a salsa business. She had no idea how to start and run a business. It was tough going for a while. Later on at one point, she was homeless, living in her car. But she was determined to learn, so she started researching. She learned how to design her own labels and create her own website. She also got a truck driver's license so she could deliver her product to stores. Cook was never in debt and eventually sold her salsa business to Campbell Soup for millions.

There is so much more to Cook's story, which she recounts in her book *Mindful Success*. Her sheer determination to reach her goals, which is rooted in her belief in herself, is so remarkable. How she overcame challenge after challenge was truly inspiring. It just goes to show anything is possible when you believe in yourself, have determination, and have a goal/vision in sight. Cook had a strong will to succeed. Her belief in herself was stronger than the fear.

244 WHAT AM I TO DO NOW?

Confidence is always up to you. It has nothing to do with your circumstances. Confidence comes from putting yourself out there in the unknown and moving forward afraid. Confidence comes from courage.

"Faith sees the invisible, believes the
unbelievable, and receives the impossible."

— Corrie Ten Boom

Sometimes, we can lose focus of ourselves without realizing it. There can be a fine line between caring for others and losing ourselves to others. Mothers definitely know that is true. I'll never forget coming home with our new baby and sitting in my cozy rocking chair with her. A good friend, who had three children herself, called to congratulate us. She told me to read *Babywise* (a must read for new parents). She also said this about being a new parent, "It's not about you anymore." And dang was that true!

Becoming a parent is a beautiful and awesome experience. It's also very humbling because life isn't all about you anymore. All the attention shifts to this tiny human being who is counting on you for everything.

The other humbling part is you have total influence over this young, developing, and vulnerable little being who is watching your every move and listening to your every word. On top of it, you're overwhelmed, so it's so easy to lose yourself in parenthood.

Much later, I realized the saying should be, "It's not *just* about you anymore." Our kids are watching us, and when we tell them to believe in themselves, to just be themselves, we should truly be demonstrating that we believe in ourselves. When we are living our life as authentically as we were meant to, our kids see that and have a point of reference and something to aspire to. This idea took me a long time to really appreciate. As Les Brown said, "You have to *be* the message you bring."

When you have a strong desire for something that aligns with your core values that excites and scares you at the same time, that's your dream, your vision of what lights you up and motivates you to grow. This not only serves as your compass, but as an anchor to your ground conviction, courage, and strength. This is where purpose comes to life and your truth is brought forth to blossom into whatever is next for you. Being authentic is just that, allowing the truth of who you really are to reveal itself in the world. Your belief in yourself comes from focusing on this truth of yours. You trust yourself because you know yourself. You know what you believe at your core.

"Your success depends mainly upon what you think of yourself and whether you believe in yourself."

— William J. H. Boetcker

We are all made up of energy and have energy all around us. Remember, energy flows where your attention goes, so you want to focus on what you want, not on what you don't want. Whatever seed (thought/belief) you plant in your mind is what will grow and manifest. Focus increases the amplitude of vibration. Your inner voice transmits the highest vibration in you. Your subconscious is programed by whatever you tell yourself, which it takes as truth. It doesn't distinguish right or wrong, good or bad—it just takes in whatever you feed it and turns it into what you believe.

That's why you need to believe in yourself. Don't wait for others to believe in you. They will not believe in you until you first believe in yourself. Belief is about trust, so believing in yourself is about trusting yourself. Since everything starts in thought, and you think in images, you want to create a positive image of yourself, which then gives your mind a positive image to believe in. This is why continuing to update your self-image is crucial. When you see it, feel it, and believe it, you become it.

> *"The only obstacle to your success and achievement is your own thought or mental image."*
>
> — Dr. Joseph Murphy

You, like everyone else, have a magnificent spirit within. You have a human body, but understand that you are not your human body. Your body is a shell holding your essence, which is who you truly are at your core. Your self is this beautiful soul that lives inside you and has unlimited, awesome potential. If you see yourself as awesome, you will feel awesome. And if you see and feel yourself as awesome, you will be awesome. What do you want to believe about yourself? What do you actually believe?

Download this affirmation to your subconscious mind:

MY AWESOMENESS CREED

I embody this magnificent, unlimited, incredible power of mind-blowing awesomeness, which is the light inside me, my spirit. And I've been given free will to choose what I will do or not do with my awesomeness. The first step is to allow myself to become aware of my truth—that awesomeness lives inside of me no matter who I am or where I come from. And only I can realize and step into that awesomeness every day. I will do this by putting it on and *being* it.

I will:

- Be **A**uthentic and true to what lights me up.
- Be **W**illing to learn while keeping an open mind.
- Be **E**mpowered in thinking, holding firm to my core beliefs.
- Be **S**uccess-minded with a winner's attitude.
- Be **O**ptimistic with hope and confidence about the future.
- Be **M**otivated and continue to stimulate interest and curiosity.
- Be **E**nthusiastic and eager, driven by deep desire.
- Be **N**imble and ready to adapt quickly and easily.
- Be **E**xpectant that something good is coming.
- Be **S**pirited and full of energy in all I do.
- Be **S**trong and grounded in my worth and ability.

Decide for your *self* today. Lean into your truth and ignite your awesomeness by trusting in yourself, the spirit breathing in you. Start building a new belief, one that sparks the light in you, the authentic you.

"Once you start believing in yourself, anything is possible.
Once you start believing in yourself, your dreams take shape.
The more you believe, the more you achieve."

— Martina Navratilova

Inspired Insight:

_____

_____

_____

_____

Inspired Action:

_____

_____

_____

_____

"I believe ambition is not a dirty word. It's just believing in yourself and your abilities. Imagine this: What would happen if we were all brave enough to believe in our own ability? To be a little bit more ambitious? I think the world would change."

— Reese Witherspoon

CHAPTER 19

CHOOSING HAPPINESS AND FINDING FULFILLMENT

"What you get by achieving your goals is not as important as what you become by achieving your goals."

— Henry David Thoreau

Happiness and fulfillment tend to be used together and are often looked at as a set. And yet, they really are distinct thoughts. Though all kind of things can make you happy—reaching a goal, getting a promotion, earning an award, winning a game, losing weight, completing a project—that kind of happiness on its own can be fleeting. Most people don't walk around energized by a goal they hit twelve months ago—that intensity passes with time. That is because happiness is a state of being. You decide to be happy or unhappy every day.

Maxwell Maltz said happiness doesn't lie in the future, but in the present. He pointed out, "It's a mental attitude, a mental habit, and if it is not learned and practiced in the present, it is never experienced."

Understand that happiness is inside work. It doesn't depend on what's going on outside of ourselves. It's not about things, but about thoughts, ideas, and attitudes. We actually think and perform better when we have a happy state of being.

Happiness is always a choice and can become a habit if you practice it enough. And when it becomes a habit, it will become of way of *being*.

> *"Happiness, true happiness, is an inner quality. It is a state of mind. If your mind is at peace, you are happy. If your mind is at peace, but you have nothing else, you can be happy. If you have everything the world can give—pleasure, possessions, power— but lack peace of mind, you can never be happy."*
>
> — Dada Vaswani

Fulfillment is even deeper than happiness. Fulfillment comes when our work (our creative expression) connects directly to what is most meaningful to us. It's something reached through time and effort. Fulfillment is when how we choose to spend our time and energy aligns with what lights us up inside and inevitably allows us to make the contribution we were intended to make in this precious life of ours on mother earth.

Your purpose is linked directly to fulfillment. This is why it is so important to tap into what truly motivates and inspires you. Your dream is who you are at your core. Your dream is aligned with your fulfillment. Your life was designed to be all about following your dreams. When you go for your dream, you are actually doing what you were put on this earth to do.

Our dreams ignite us, scare us, challenge us, teach us, connect us, and cause us to grow. Through achieving our dreams, we evolve into our next best version.

When you go for a big goal that's deeply important to you at the soul level, you will know fulfillment. Fulfillment comes from doing what you love and giving back in ways that matter. Focus on the dream that is calling you every day. It is the foundation and heart core where you'll find meaning, purpose, and fulfillment.

"Goal setting is the most important aspect of all improvement and personal development plans. It is the key to all fulfillment and achievement."

— Paul J. Meyer

Your work in the world, whether in a for-profit or nonprofit, writing a book, creating a program or spearheading a campaign, working with a charity or volunteering, is where you have the opportunity to connect, inspire, and make the world better. Everyone wants to feel significant, loved, and appreciated. Making an inspired positive difference in people's lives by doing something that was really important to you is the most fulfilling thing you can do. It's your contribution to the world, which is ignited through your dreams and talents.

Whatever is truly calling you is what you were created to do. You were designed to continue to grow and you were given free will to choose how you grow. I watched my big sister Marie take her last breath at just fifty. We don't know how much time we have, so don't waste it. Lean into your life, and do what gives you life. Follow the spark that ignites your soul and invigorates your mind and body. Every day is an opportunity to tap into that amplified aliveness!

> *"Success is not just making money. Success is happiness.*
> *Success is fulfillment; it's the ability to give."*
>
> — Adam Neumann

I watched Harlene, a former colleague and dear friend, evolve into a happy and fulfilling life doing work she absolutely loves. When she officially retired in her mid-sixties, she started doing volunteer work. Harlene always saw herself as a connector. She identified with the role because she loved people and helping them make connections. When she retired (or tried to at least), she volunteered in her community by delivering meals on wheels and helping in various ways within the senior community.

An opportunity to make memory bears out of the clothes of loved ones who had passed away presented itself. Harlene had never done this before, but it sounded interesting and would provide a meaningful memento for those who had lost someone. She knew how to sew and decided she was up for the challenge. She did not know at the time it would end up being some of the most fulfilling work she'd ever done. And it took her "connector" role to a whole new level (updated self-image).

Through making the bears, Harlene connected people with deep, beautiful memories of loved ones. The process became very personal for her. Each bear had a story to be shared and remembered. She met a whole new community of heart-centered people, some who've become dear friends. She's been featured in local newspapers and magazines. She never thought about going into business when she retired, but it happened organically. Harlene says when she is working on a bear, something inside of her just takes over, and effortlessly, she knows exactly how she will design it.

Harlene is clear these are Bears to Cherish, which became her company's name. Her personal journey with the bears has been so transforming to see. It connected her to something so deep, purposeful, and fulfilling. She even sees herself as an artist now (updated self-image).

Harlene eventually expanded her bears beyond memorializing loved ones to also celebrating people and their interests. She is truly making a unique and special contribution to the world. And she's connected her bear customers as they share their beautiful memories of the loved ones they've lost, helping them heal as a community. What a beautiful legacy for someone who has embraced happiness and found joy and fulfillment by brightening the lives of families throughout the country.

> *"When you have balance in your life, work becomes an entirely different experience. There is a passion that moves you to a whole new level of fulfillment and gratitude, and that's when you can do your best…for yourself and for others."*
>
> — Cara Delevingne

I was blessed when my hairdresser recommended Otto, my contractor. He wasn't like any contractor I had ever met. He actually does a lot of the work himself along with one helper. Otto said he used to have twelve people working for him, but he found better balance in working as a smaller outfit. First of all, he's truly a fine artist. He loves art and drawing, and he studies all the greats. He's creative, curious, and always looking through the lens of what's possible, and all that informs his work as a contractor.

Otto is also the calmest contractor I've ever met. He doesn't let much bother him. Anyone who's done any significant construction knows there will always be challenges. It's like pulling a loose thread—once you start to pull it, more unravels. But as problems popped up, Otto would calmly say, "That's okay; we'll figure it out." And we always did.

What struck me with Otto was he seemed to find joy in whatever he was doing at the time. Though he would love to have more time to spend on his art, he said he also finds pleasure in the work he does for his clients. He chooses to bring the same creativity that inspires him in his fine art to his work when transforming people's homes. All of the work he does is truly a labor of love for his art.

"You do not find the happy life. You make it."

— Camilla Eyring Kimball

Otto is currently building a studio in his garage. He works on it late at night, after a hard day's work on construction sites. He told me he wanted to do this for quite a while, but he couldn't seem to find the time until he became aware of a pattern in how he was living. After work, he would go home, have dinner, and watch television. He pretty much did that every day. Then it hit him that if he didn't change his living pattern, he'd never get his dream workspace. He decided to just start. He stopped watching TV as often and started working on his studio little by little at night and when he finds extra time on the weekend. And he's enjoying the process!

Many nights, Otto is tired, so it would be easy for him to make excuses not to work on his studio. But his burning desire keeps him focused, and somehow, he finds the energy. Otto's dream studio is constantly moving closer to being realized.

In the meantime, Otto finds the stimulation and inspiration every day in the work he does on people's homes. He still gets to use his imagination and creativity on every project, while he continues to bring about his dream studio. Otto has learned to weave his passion and creativity into both his personal and professional lives. He feels happy and fulfilled in both environments. It makes sense because he's aligned who he is at his core—an artist—with his entire life.

Understand that Otto made a conscious choice that also allows him to enjoy the process. Plus, Otto is very grateful for how far he has come from his early life in Guatemala. He's transformed his home into his own little paradise, which he shares with his wife and two children. He doesn't sweat the bumps in the road; rather, he sees the challenges as opportunities to use his creativity to solve problems.

Otto has learned the true power of perception—life is what you make it. And he's chosen to make his a life of happiness and fulfillment—while on his journey to making his dreams come true—all in a day's work.

"But what is happiness except the simple harmony
between a man and the life he leads?"

— Albert Camus

It's so important to *make the time* to connect with what's most important to you and to embrace the dreams that inspire you. Then immediately look at how you can start weaving some element of what lights you up into your life right now and into each day. It's how your dreams can serve you in aligning with a life that's rich with happiness and fulfillment. Let your dreams inspire and *ignite* ideas, giving fuel to your emotions, building momentum around those inspired ideas. Then get moving! Take inspired imperfect action every day—allowing those ideas to become your new reality, and enjoy the process along the way. When those around you see your transformation, watch how you can inspire them while on your own journey. There's nothing more powerful to inspire and motivate others than someone who walks their talk. You don't have to convince them of anything because they see the evidence in your results and in *you*. When you *say* anything is possible, that can be inspiring. But when you *show them* anything is possible, look out world! That's life changing and very impactful! That's leading by example. There's nothing more gratifying and affirming than having a positive influence on another individual. That's a legacy that every single one of us should aspire for in this precious lifetime. Live your truth, be grateful, and give back along the way.

"It is not in the pursuit of happiness that we find

fulfillment, it is in the happiness of pursuit."

— Denis Waitley

Inspired Insight:

_____

_____

_____

_____

Inspired Action:

_____

_____

_____

_____

"A life of fulfillment comes from within, through the knowledge that you were created with everything you need to be happy."

— Deepak Chopra

?

CHAPTER 20

LIVING A VISION-DRIVEN LIFE

"If you are working on something exciting that you really care about, you don't have to be pushed. The vision pulls you."

— Steve Jobs

What exactly is "a vision-driven life"? It's a life led by your vision, the dreams of what you would absolutely love to create and how you are driven to make the world a better place. It is a life created by your specific design—your personal blueprint and where you focus every day using your powerful mental faculty, your will. Understand that your vision is your compass, inspired by and led through the lens of your dream.

The alternative? Living a condition-driven life. A condition-driven life is created by default; it's not designed by you, but instead determined by outside circumstances and conditions. It has no compass. It is as if you're a pinball, aimlessly being flung in all sorts of directions—not really being led, but pushed by the gravity of the outside world. Where does that actually lead you? Everywhere and nowhere. It is utter confusion, and it is why, before you can know where you're heading, you have to know what you want. You need something to aim at—a big, beautiful, inspired possibility. You need a vision!

"Vision is a destination—a fixed point to which we focus all effort.
Strategy is a route—an adaptable path to get us where we want to go."

— Simon Sinek

Steve Jobs talked about connecting the dots in our lives. Our incredible mental faculty called our memory helps us to do this by reflecting and recalling. Jobs said we can only connect the dots looking backward, not forward. That is because the future is unknown. But there is also another part of memory we can tap into—future memory. We do this by putting on a future image of what we would love. Remember our subconscious mind doesn't know the difference between what is real or imagined. We are conditioning our memory for the future by stepping into our new self-image and acting *as if* with behaviors that match our next best version. And when we look forward, belief must kick in.

If you think about it, you choose how you will see your future with another awesome mental faculty, your perception—is the glass half-full or half-empty? Your dream can be realized or fade away. Will you let fear lead you, or will you let faith lead you? Both require you to believe in something you cannot see. Your journey on this earth is for developing, evolving, and continuing to grow until you take your last breath. The compass leading the way is the bright vision you create from the awesomeness that lives inside you. Trust in that. Align with that. And allow yourself to realize that by listening to your beautiful mental faculty, your intuition.

You are supposed to be the star in your life's script. You are also the director of the movie called *Your Life*. Dream audaciously and big! Let the life inside of you be expressed by you in this world. Let your vision guide your life, not your circumstances and conditions. Those may be your facts at the moment, but they most definitely aren't your truth.

"Vision is the art of seeing what is invisible to others."

— Jonathan Swift

Living a vision-driven life is about allowing the authentic you to be the light illuminating the path of your life. The outside doesn't have a role in your movie. Use your marvelous mental faculty called reason to choose specific thoughts that inspire the life and light inside you. You decide what, who, where, how much, and how big it can be. Don't take the normal way and let what's outside control your life. Don't live a condition-driven life. Don't operate strictly by the five senses. Look deeper than what you can see, hear, taste, smell, and touch. You have these genius power tools, your mental faculties, inside of you to help you navigate through your outside conditions and limiting paradigms. Don't give the outside world the starring role in your life-script. Cut that scene out and replace it with something you want, something that lights you up inside and lights up your soul.

When you allow yourself to connect with that deeper part of you, your awesomeness, you will be heading down a path of joy, happiness, and fulfillment.

> *"Your time is limited, so don't waste it living someone else's life. Don't be trapped by dogma—which is living with the results of other people's thinking. Don't let the noise of others' opinions drown out your own inner voice. And most important, have the courage to follow your heart and intuition."*
>
> — Steve Jobs

I've referenced Mary Morrissey in this book. I've quoted her and shared things I've learned from her as a mentor. I received my two coaching certifications from her Life Mastery Institute, now called The Brave

Thinking Institute. She introduced me to the power of living a vision-driven life. It is my hope that this book ignites the same in you.

"Dreaming, after all, is a form of planning."

— Gloria Steinem

A successful business starts with a business plan. A successful life starts with a life plan. This is your vision of what you would love to do/have in all areas of your life—your health and wellbeing, your relationships, your vocation/creative expression/work and your time/financial freedom. All areas intersect and contribute to a fulfilling and joyful life. But only you can think up and plan this life—and you do so using your amazing mental faculty, your imagination.

Every dream starts as a thought before it comes into form. What are you focusing on? Remember, where your attention goes, your energy flows.

Ask yourself empowering questions like: What's important to me? What do I want more of? What do I want less of? What would I absolutely love my life to look like? How would I love to feel? Let that be the root and foundation you build a beautiful and awesome life on. Let that inspiring dream serve as the lighthouse when life sends you into the stormy sea and throws you off course.

When you know where you're heading, and you are grounded and fueled with the deep awareness of why you're heading there, your vision will keep you moving forward toward the joyful and fulfilling life you've designed.

"Imagination is the beginning of creation. You imagine what you desire;
you will what you imagine; and at last, you create what you will."

— George Bernard Shaw

Inspired Insight:

_____

_____

_____

_____

Inspired Action:

_____

_____

_____

_____

"We are not stuck in the ruts of destiny; we have the power to break free, clear our vision, and see a new life for ourselves."

— Tony Clark

A FINAL NOTE

IGNITING YOUR WHAT'S NEXT EVOLUTION

Now that you've finished this book and have been introduced to the Seven Step IgniteU System, it's time to take center stage in your life!

No more excuses—that's procrastination due to fear. Stop settling—that's just another form of giving up and a distraction due to fear. Drop the victim mindset of "poor me" and replace it with an empowering mindset of "*Why not me?*" Walk your talk. Be a role model by living what *you* believe. Step into the spotlight of your life. Allow your AWESOMENESS to shine through. Listen to where your soul is directing you. What would you really love to manifest and create in your life? Embrace the possibilities. What's an action you can take right now from where you are? Try new things. Do it afraid. Be okay with falling down. It's how you learn new things. Stretch yourself with the goals you set. Believe you can and let go of the self-sabotaging voice of why you can't. It's destructive and has no place with you on center stage. Pay attention to who you spend your time with, and don't waste it with toxic people.

You've got one life, and it's up to you what you do with that life. The choices you make, the people you hang out with, the food you eat, the movies and shows you watch, the books you read, the music and podcasts you listen to, the social media you engage in, how you take care of yourself, what you spend your money on, what time you wake up in the morning and what time you go to bed are all up to you. The power of your life is in your hands. You decide what you do with that power. Now take a deep breath and allow your mind to do a reset.

First and foremost, do you have a clear and defined vision that lights you up, is important to you, and aligns with your core beliefs? If not, it's time to take that imperfect inspired action step right now. Go through the IgniteU System again in Chapters 6-12. Get clear with a big bodacious goal—a beautiful vision that's sparking your soul's desire. And if you do have a vision that's firing you up inside, then what's an imperfect inspired action step that you can take today to move you closer to your goal? Remember, **Action Changes Things.** Nothing changes until you make a move.

Next, put your stake in the ground and make a committed decision to continue to take an imperfect inspired action every day. One small move a day will add up to a whole lot of action in the course of a month. In the lines below, list ten inspired actions that you will commit to taking in service of your vision within the next thirty days.

Ten Inspired Actions:

1. _____
2. _____
3. _____
4. _____
5. _____
6. _____
7. _____
8. _____
9. _____
10. _____

As discussed in Chapter 9, having a support system around you and partner(s) in believing is key to keeping you accountable and on track with your vision. Think about who that person might be for you. Whom do you admire? Who has success in an area of your life that you respect? What are some of their habits and behaviors? Reach out to them. Have coffee with them or take them to lunch. You'd be surprised how open people are to sharing their wisdom with someone who is inspired to grow, willing to listen, open to exploring new ideas, eager to learn, and prepared to take action.

If you haven't already, start a gratitude journal as I suggested in Chapter 11. Every morning when you wake up and every evening before you lay your head down to sleep, write down something you are grateful for. It doesn't matter how small it is. Just don't miss this opportunity to connect with gratitude. Remember, it's a high-frequency vibration, and it's in alignment with the frequency of abundance.

Finally, allow yourself to fuse with an updated self-image of the person in your vision. The person who is doing new things to stretch you into your next best version of the awesome individual who is deserving of a life that ignites your soul! Understand that what you think, you become. *Be* the *superstar* of your own life as you step onto your life's stage and own it!

In this book, you learned the importance of having an inspired aiming point for your life—a vision, the power of your soul's purpose, and the importance of having a *what's possible* mindset when using your imagination to create a life that you love. You learned the value of blessing and releasing anything that isn't serving your vision and how important it is to always *be* the leader of your own life by trusting your inner voice and wisdom. You learned about seeing fear and failure as a requirement to learn and grow from rather than a weak identity to accept and contract into. You gained the understanding that you matter and are deserving of a life you love and are inspired by, and that you have one life and it's waiting for you—if you are open to it.

If you decide for a vision that lights you up and aligns with what's most important to you, and if you will trust in the AWESOME spirit that's breathing you and follow the path that's calling you, you will find joy and fulfillment. And the world will be better because of you.

Dance into the spotlight of your life and *be* the leading lady/man of an awesome life script. It may be time for a rewrite, or maybe it's time for your sequel. Make it one that lights your soul on fire. Your stage is set and ready for you to ignite your *what's next evolution*!

Quiet on set…

Lights…

Camera…

Action!

I'd love to hear from you and learn what inspired insights you had after reading my book. What came up for you as you considered new possibilities for a vision-driven life? What obstacles or challenges have been keeping you stuck and stopping you from going for your dream? I'd love to help you step into your what's next evolution and create a vision-driven plan that sparks your authentic light inside. I would like to offer you a complimentary, no-obligation, 30-60 minute consultation by phone, by Zoom, or in person (if geography allows) to see how I can assist you....

My email address is Patti@PattiSmithCoaching.com and my Instagram is @pattismithcoaching. Please email me or direct message me with your name and time zone so we can schedule your complimentary consultation.

Here's to your success in your next starring role!

Patti Smith

"With realization of one's own potential and self-confidence in one's ability, one can build a better world."

— Dalai Lama

?

ABOUT THE AUTHOR

Patti Smith is a professional keynote speaker, an innovative entrepreneur, and a life success coach who passionately believes in the power of human potential. She has two certifications from the Life Mastery Institute, now called the Brave Thinking Institute, the premier training center for transformational coaching.

Patti's career encompasses experience gained within the fashion industry, publishing field, and luxury market. Her achievements in sales and sales management have garnered her multiple awards.

The deep personal impact of serving as primary caregiver to her sister, whom she subsequently lost to cancer in the prime of life, first caused a focused shift for her into the field of healthcare. Patti was eventually led to an entrepreneurial firm specializing in technology solutions for seniors and the disabled. She served as VP of Relational Partnerships, bringing in thirteen partners, and in less than two years, she was promoted to President.

Patti continued to follow her passion for helping people, and in 2016, she made a shift to the personal development field and opened Patti Smith Innovative Coaching, LLC.

Patti lives in southern California with her husband of nearly twenty-five years and their two dogs. She and her husband have a beautiful, bright, and very driven daughter who is now in college, pursing her dream in entertainment business management.

?

BOOK PATTI SMITH TO SPEAK AT YOUR NEXT EVENT

As a passionate speaker and success coach in the personal development arena, Patti Smith works with organizations and individuals, helping them focus and get clear on their goals, build healthier relationships, accelerate their results, and achieve success from the inside out.

Understanding that most people use only a fraction of the potential they have locked inside of themselves, Patti has made it her mission to help people ignite and optimize their human potential. This mission is the core foundation in her trainings, talks, and workshops.

Whether it's a twenty-minute talk, a half-day workshop, a corporate training, or a motivating keynote speech, your group, organization, or company will be inspired, ignited, and impacted by Patti's message. If you are looking for a memorable speaker who will leave your audience wanting more, book Patti Smith today!

To discuss with Patti how she can IGNITE your audience, contact her at:

Patti@PattiSmithCoaching.com

?

PATTI SMITH INNOVATIVE COACHING

Achieve new heights of success, confidence, and fulfillment by creating a vision-driven mindset and life plan with an experienced life success coach!

For most of her adult life, Patti Smith has been studying and implementing transformational success principles. In the process, she earned two coaching certificates and spent years studying personal development and its application. This journey has given her the insight and ability to achieve many of her own dreams, both professionally and personally. She walks her talk.

Patti can provide you with the support and accountability you need as she guides you through simple, proven and powerful success systems that will spark and IGNITE your authentic light and genius. The end result will be having the tools and confidence you need to step into your next best version and own it!

The only thing required is a good attitude, an open mind, a willingness to invest in yourself, and the courage to take imperfect action.

To schedule a thirty-minute complimentary consultation and learn more about Patti's coaching services, visit her website:

www.PattiSmithCoaching.com